WHY CHRISTIANS BURN OUT

WHY CHRISTIANS BURN OUT

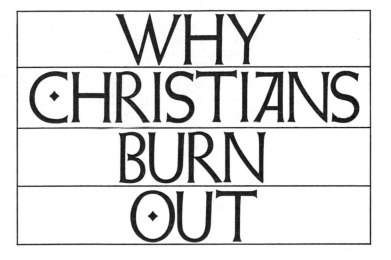

CHARLES E. PERRY, JR.

THOMAS NELSON PUBLISHERS
Nashville • Camden • New York

Published in Nashville, Tennessee, by Thomas Nelson, Inc. and distributed in Canada by Lawson Falle, Ltd., Cambridge, Ontario. Printed in the United States of America.

Unless otherwise indicated, Scripture quotations are from the King James Version of the Bible. Scripture quotations marked RSV are from the Revised Standard Version.

Material quoted on pages 25–6 is reprinted by permission of the Harvard Business Review. Excerpt from "When Executives Burn Out" by Harry Levinson (HBR, May/June 1981). Copyright © 1981 by the President and Fellows of Harvard College; all rights reserved.

Material quoted on pages 96–9 is from *Type A Behavior and Your Heart*, by Meyer M. Friedman, M.D., and Ray H. Rosenman, M.D. Copyright © 1974 by Meyer Friedman. Reprinted by permission of Alfred A. Knopf, Inc.

Material quoted on pages 101–3 is an excerpt from BURN OUT: The High Cost of High Achievement by Dr. Herbert J. Freudenberger, Ph.D. Copyright © 1980 by Herbert J. Freudenberger, Ph.D. and Geraldine Richelson. Reprinted by permission of Doubleday & Company, Inc.

Material quoted on pages 114–7 is from J. L. Barkas, *The Help Book*. Copyright © 1979 by J. L. Barkas. (New York: Charles Scribner's Sons, 1979). Reprinted with permission of Charles Scribner's Sons.

Second printing

Library of Congress Cataloging in Publication Data

Perry, Charles E.
  Why Christians burn out.

  Includes bibliographical references.
  1. Clergy—Psychology. 2. Clergy—Job stress.
3. Burnout (Psychology) 4. Church officers—Psychology. 5. Church officers—Job stress.
I. Title.
BV4398.P47   253'.2   82-2098
ISBN 0-8407-5800-6   AACR2

To my faithful wife, Martha. Her encouragement, perseverance in typing the manuscript, and enduring love for its author has made this book possible.

Contents

Acknowledgments

Many people have given their time, experiences, and skills to make this book possible. I am indebted to them all. I would like to thank each one by name but that would be impossible. My gratitude is extended to all the people who have suffered burnout and shared their stories with me. I thank you with all my heart. You have given life to this book.

Authors Mary Beth Moster and Norman B. Rohrer devoted many hours to reading and commenting on the manuscript. Their help was greatly appreciated.

I also wish to thank Peter Gillquist and the staff of Thomas Nelson Publishers for their personal concern in helping this new author. Their extra efforts have made the rough road of getting published a little smoother.

Most of all, I wish to thank my parents, especially my mother. Her writings, which impressed me as a youth, encouraged me throughout this project.

1

Something Is Wrong!

On a hot evening in July, Pastor Bill Pennington*
sat before his tiny congregation. He waited for the
song leader to finish the last hymn prior to the beginning of the message.

His eyes glanced back and forth at the empty pews
and the handful of people. He recalled the past ten
extremely difficult years of labor among these people.
He was just thirty-five when he was called to serve as
the spiritual leader of this flock. Those ten years had
also been filled with many blessings. Bill's family had
job security, a good home, and food on the table.
Their pay had always been small, but God had given
them what they needed—and He had provided the
extra money for the two Pennington children to go to
college.

Bill had thought that his problem would be solved
now that the money stress concerning college expenses was over. But it remained. The headaches,

---

*Names of individuals interviewed by the author have
been changed throughout this book.

exhaustion, and depression seemed to get worse. Whenever problems arose in the church, Bill came home with a sick and fatigued look in his eyes. His wife, Louise, could always read the stress on his face. She tried to be an encouragement to Bill, even when smiling was difficult. Quite often when Bill became discouraged, depressed, and ill, she began to feel the same way. Louise saw an important part of her life slipping away. She did not know what to do about it. The days of crying and periods of depression became more frequent for Louise as she saw her husband suffering.

Bill also was experiencing more and more migraine headaches. Sometimes he had to come home and lie down in a dark room for two or three hours to find relief. One day, after a discouraging church board meeting, a new problem developed. As he left the meeting, his stomach began churning, his knees felt weak, and Bill began vomiting. *"What is wrong with me?"* he thought.

He went to his family doctor to find help for what he believed was a physical ailment. His doctor prescribed some antidepressants to help Bill get out of the slump he was in. Bill took the pills for one week, then threw them away because of their side effects.

Several weeks later there was a discipline problem in the church. The stress was more than Bill could bear. The Wednesday night business meeting was a shouting match. Some were taking sides while others were trying to be objective. The whole matter was tabled until after the next Sunday evening service.

Bill's mind was brought quickly to the present

hour, as he heard the song leader introduce the special music before the message. It was almost time to stand behind the pulpit as he had hundreds of times before, but this time he knew something was wrong. His head was spinning, and his stomach was churning in a way he had never experienced before. He knew he was going to be sick. The thought of another business meeting later in the evening like the last one on Wednesday made him feel worse by the minute. Finally Bill jotted a note—"I am sick. Dismiss the service"—handed it to the song leader, and departed from the church.

That incident was the beginning of the end of Pastor Bill Pennington's work in the ministry. He soon realized that he could no longer continue in the physical distress which he suffered each week. He resigned and went into the used car business.

Bill Pennington's crisis is not unique among ministers, nor among productive Christian men and women in general. I, and many of my pastoral colleagues, have experienced the pangs of burnout, as have countless people in other lines of work. Perhaps burnout is a reality you are confronting just now.

A thirty-six-year-old Chicago elementary school teacher lets student teachers run her class. She says, "Some days I can't bear to go to school. My legs won't take me to the classroom." After thirteen years of teaching, she is looking for a job in public relations.[1]

A twenty-eight-year-old woman, with a master's degree in family planning and public health, left her two-year career with a family planning clinic and became a carpenter. Her burnout experience was so severe that she could no longer work in a job associated with her raining.

A forty-five-year-old business executive found himself in a corporate structure which locked him into a position with little authority, no chance of promotion, and unrealistic expectations by his employer. He quit his fifty-thousand-dollar-per-year executive job, sold his home and most of his belongings, and moved to the Adirondack Mountains to operate a general store.

These people are only a few of the many troubled ones who come to a point in their careers when they can no longer contend with the crushing weight of the stress in their occupations.

In 1977 the American Psychological Association announced a symposium on the topic of burnout at its annual convention. The symposium was presented in a room that seated two hundred, but the subject matter was so popular there was no standing room and a large group gathered outside just to listen.[2]

A University of Michigan graduate student gave a seminar on burnout at a conference in Chicago for crisis center administrators. Shortly after her talk, she began receiving calls from agencies all over Illinois asking her to come to do workshops on the subject.[3]

What is it that causes people to throng to these seminars? What are people feeling inside as they desperately seek answers? A former pastor from Ohio shared his feelings of failure, disappointment, and discouragement, after he resigned and left the ministry because of an overbearing senior pastor.

14

At home I had all the empty hours in the day to face. I did not know what to do with myself. I had understood myself in terms of being a minister, now it was not there [sic]. Perhaps it was that being a minister had always been an easy way to relate to people. There were so many built-in responses. It was a way of being with people. But now it was over, I wondered where the separation was between my life as a minister and my life as a person, and I wondered if the one was strong enough to exist without the other. Now my pulpit robe hung in the closet. I would wake up in the morning wondering what I was going to do with all the hours which waited for me; the empty, long, frightful hours of sadness and grief. I had no job, but what seemed worse, I had no structure to give limits or meaning to my life. I felt adrift.[4]

What is this malady which suddenly seems to have hit our modern society?

Tired From "People-Work"

Psychologists have begun to study this phenomenon in recent years. One article defined burnout as

. . . a syndrome of emotional exhaustion and cynicism that occurs frequently among individuals who do "people-work" of some kind. A key aspect of the burnout syndrome is increased feelings of emotional exhaustion. As their emotional resources are depleted, workers feel they are no longer able to give of themselves at a psychological level.[5]

People who do people work are usually educated for their jobs—teachers, social workers, managers, pastors. Hence, burnout is not a subject to boast about. It is equated with failure and supposedly reflects on one's ability to perform well the profession one chose. Most professional workers are aware of tremendous peer pressure. That pressure is sometimes more than the professional can stand. Colleagues whisper, "I thought he was more stable than to just throw his career away." "Some people have it and some don't." "The weak just don't make it in this business. It's the survival of the fittest."

Comments such as these, and others far more cutting, have caused some burnout victims to question their own stability. The conclusion is usually some form of self-condemnation. This guilt has left many thousands of professional people with a burden they cannot bear. Finding oneself detesting a job is devastating when sixteen to twenty years and thousands of dollars have been spent preparing for that career.

What are the symptoms of burning out of a career in which you have invested most of your life? The first tell-tale sign is often apathy, which quickly affects the quality of work done. The list can grow to low morale, absenteeism, frequent job changes, alcohol and drug abuse, marital and family conflicts, and psychological problems.

Most of all, burnout leaves a person adrift in a sea of mixed emotions. Many people in the early stages of burnout express a feeling of futility in that job which had once seemed so promising. No longer do they feel they can really help others. Gone is the anticipation for promotions, salary increases, and

new challenges. Those who burnout and remain on
the job consider every addition to their work as the
straw which might break their backs. Those who
burnout and resign are no better off. The psychological anguish of a meaningless life causes as much,
if not more, pain and suffering than being under the
stress of the former career. The stress on the job is
unbearable, but the feelings of guilt, failure, self-
condemnation, and futility make resignation un-
thinkable.

Many professionals have had much help to achieve
the positions they hold. Wives have sacrificed those
tender years with the children to work and put
"hubby" through his schooling. Fathers and mothers
have scrimped and saved to help their sons and
daughters train for that dream career. The children
are proud of daddy's career and are not ashamed to
let others know their daddy is a success. Community
leaders and neighbors look up to and count on the
professional for his expertise in community problems. He is a success in everybody's eyes except his
own. He knows that he will break if something isn't
done before long. How can he disappoint all those
people? How could he ever face them if he resigned
and left his career?

I believe that those in "full-time Christian work"
face the heaviest decisions in the matter of burnout.
When a pastor or missionary or youth leader burns
out and leaves the ministry, he disappoints not only
his wife, his children, his parents, his congregation,
fellow pastors, seminary professors, and the whole
denomination. He believes he surely has dis-
appointed *God!*

Hired by God

Most Christian workers believe their work is more than a job; it is a *ministry*. Lay people can speak freely of job and career changes, but such a subject is not to be broached by one of God's "called" servants. (The same difficult circumstances apply if a Christian believes he or she has been given a talent or called into a secular job by God.)

Ultimately, the issue of "the calling of God" is what troubles Christian workers who burn out and leave the ministry. Most believe that God has called them into some form of lifetime service. To leave that ministry is in essence saying, "I don't care what God wants for me." Ministers, missionaries, and youth workers who burn out and leave a ministry are looked upon as weak in faith, carnal, out of fellowship with God, and rebellious against God's will. Some Christians even believe such people are potentially dangerous. Surely God could strike them down at any moment! So don't stand too close. A burned out Christian worker suffers severe guilt feelings after he or she leaves the ministry. Burnout victims believe they are a disappointment to everybody except Satan!

Survival of the Fittest?

When I was a college student and studying for the ministry, I had experience firsthand of watching pastors burn out.

I remember well the number of burnouts I encountered. I always thought, *They weren't strong, but I am*

*strong enough to endure all things. They must have taken
their eyes off the Lord!*

I recall the actions of one pastor who lived near our
home. Frank was thirty-five years old and married,
with three children. He was the associate pastor of a
two-hundred-fifty-member evangelical church. He
had served in that capacity for four years. Quite
evidently, he was burned out. His sermons raged
with innuendos pointed at the board and the senior
pastor. Frank's wife was not supportive of him, fear-
ing that he would lose his job and her security.

One Monday, after a vicious encounter with the
church board, Frank disappeared. Late that night his
wife filed a missing persons report with civil authorities. On Wednesday afternoon the police found
Frank's car by the city reservoir. The keys were in the
car, and Frank's shoes were at the water's edge. The
authorities searched the lake in vain for three days
and finally declared Frank dead.

I could hardly accept that a pastor would ever be so
troubled as to take his own life. Again I thought, as I
had conditioned myself to think, *He was weak.*

About a year later, a member from Frank's church
was vacationing on the West Coast. She boarded a
bus and was startled to find herself looking into the
face of her former pastor. That was the end of Frank's
charade and escape. Frank's wife divorced him, his
denomination defrocked him, and his family dis-
owned him. I have lost contact with Frank, for he
drifts from city to city like a ship without a port.

I had been conditioned to believe that if I remained
strong and had abundant faith, then I would never

experience failure in life or burnout in service to Christ and His people.

I even remember reading Second Corinthians 11:23–27 and believing that I could have stood with Paul in his trials and not wavered an inch. Paul described his trials with these words:

> Are they ministers of Christ? (I speak as a fool) I am more; in labors more abundant, in stripes above measure, in prisons more frequent, in deaths oft. Of the Jews five times received I forty stripes save one. Thrice was I beaten with rods, once was I stoned, thrice I suffered shipwreck, a night and a day I have been in the deep; In journeyings often, in perils of waters, in perils of robbers, in perils by mine own countrymen, in perils by the heathen, in perils in the city, in perils in the wilderness, in perils in the sea, in perils among false brethren; in weariness and painfulness, in watchings often, in hunger and thirst, in fastings often, in cold and nakedness.

I could do that! I could go through those kinds of trials. After all, I had the training, the strength, and the faith needed to survive!

After nine years in the pastorate I began to have second thoughts about my own ability to cope with the pastoral ministry. I had just weathered a church split and some health problems. My faith in Jesus Christ was strong, I thought, even stronger than before those trials. But for some reason, I began to lose interest in achieving great things for God in that particular ministry. I remained faithful to the work for three more years. I did the work of a pastor but had no sense of achievement as I had before.

Running on the Treadmill

Then the slightest problems began to upset me. I became critical and lacked understanding in dealing with others, although I prayed constantly that God would make me sensitive to the needs of my flock. I blamed the leadership of the church for problems which I could have prevented.

I once had a treadmill E.K.G. administered to test my heart. The doctors thought I had a heart problem, but instead found a condition caused by stress, which exhibited symptoms similar to those of a heart problem. How difficult and futile running on that treadmill was. I put forth everything I had and went nowhere. That was the basic feeling I had towards my ministry—futility!

One day it dawned on me why Frank had run away from it all. That was his way of escaping the consequences of burnout. At that point, I chose not to follow such a foolish example as Frank set. My family and brothers and sisters in Christ meant too much to me. So I endured another year.

Lesser of Two Evils

One evening I was called to the hospital. A lady in our church had been brought in for emergency surgery. As I sat in the waiting room with the family, I overheard two men talking about their problems. One was a minister and the other an insurance salesman.

The minister shared his problems openly: He had

an obstinate congregation who wanted neither changes nor responsibilities. He complained of the pressure from the superiors in his denomination to produce visible results of his ministry. He moaned about his small salary and the unpaid bills. He hung his head as he spoke of his wife's full-time job, which she had taken to help pay the bills and buy groceries. His frustration and despair were vivid as he shook his head, wondering aloud what was going to happen to him and his family.

The entire time the insurance salesman sat there, saying, "Yes . . . yes . . . I know exactly what you are going through, for I was in the ministry myself. I faced those same problems. As a matter of fact, we became so desperate for money, I took a job on the side selling insurance, just so we could pay the bills and buy food. When the church members found out I was moonlighting, they cut my salary by almost half. It was all I could take. I quit and left the ministry."

"How can you live with yourself?" the minister asked him. "How can you cope with that failure hanging over you?"

The insurance salesman answered, "It was the lesser of two evils."

I was so startled by the former pastor's remark that I turned around in my seat to see what this weakling looked like. Much to my surprise, he reminded me of myself! He carried himself in much the same manner as I did, as if he were weighted down with a heavy burden. I thought, *Will I be talking about the lesser of two evils some day?*

Something is severely wrong when a person considers his or her profession, which was once believed to be a calling from God, an evil thing in the first place. What happens to an individual when aspiration turns to hopelessness, zeal fades into listlessness, and concern lapses into carelessness? What triggers the professional to say finally, "I've had it!" Where does it all start? When do things start to change? Who's to blame? How can the damage be repaired? Is there such a thing as starting over?

The remaining chapters of this book examine the problems of burnout which any Christian can face, and how I answered these questions.

Notes

1. "Help! Teacher Can't Teach!" *Time*, June 16, 1980, p. 57.
2. Cary Cherniss, "Recent Research and Theory on Job Stress and Burnout in Helping Professions," Seminar paper presented at the University of Michigan, May 12, 1978, p. 1.
3. Ibid.
4. David W. Anderson, "Leaving," *Your Church*, July/August, 1980, p. 26. Used by permission.
5. Christina Maslach and Susan E. Jackson, "The Measurement of Experienced Burnout," *Journal of Occupational Behaviour*, Vol. 2 (1981), 99–113. Used by permission.

2
Sitting in the Ashes

"What does it feel like to be burned out?" my wife asked me one day.

"That is difficult to answer," I said. "I feel much as Job did when he was sitting in the ashes of his life's dreams."

Many years ago there lived a man named Job in the land of Uz. He was a God-fearing and morally upright citizen. He had a lovely family, a nice home, and a prosperous business. Things couldn't have been better.

Then tragedy struck. A windstorm blew down his house and killed all ten of his children. Another storm killed part of his herds. Rustlers took the rest. Then he became infected with boils from head to toe. His wife, instead of offering support and encouragement, complained bitterly. Her mumbled bickering grated on his already shattered spirit, and he retreated to a pile of ashes, regretting he had ever been born (see Job 1–3).

His friends were no help. They believed that only the wicked suffered stress and tragedy. Their lack of compassion and false accusations made Job's mental problem worse each time they visited him.

It would be inaccurate to say that Job experienced burnout. But his story is important to us because many of the symptoms are the same. He certainly suffered the compounding of much stress and grief in a very short time. Had it not been for Job's faith in God, through all his testing, he would have died of self-pity while sitting in the ashes.

Many people are sitting in the ashes of an incinerated career and doubting if there is anything left to live for. The experience of burnout is such a tragedy that many of its victims turn to hate the professions they once loved. Some victims of extreme burnout curse the day they were born and consider life not worth living! Usually, burnout victims end up despising their jobs, other people, and themselves. Here is how one corporate executive tells his story:

In March of 1963, I moved to a small town in Iowa with my wife and son of four weeks. I was an up-and-coming engineer with the electric company—magic and respected words in those days.

Ten years later things had changed. When we went to social gatherings and talked to people, I ended up having to defend the electric company. At the time we were tying into a consortium, which was building a nuclear generating plant. The amount of negative criticism was immense, and it never really let up. Refusing to realize how important that generating plant was to a reliable flow of electricity, people continued to find fault.

Now, nearly ten years later, we are under even

greater attack. In my present role, I'm the guy who catches it all. I can't seem to get people to stand still and listen, and I can't continue to take all the hostility that goes with it—the crank calls, being woken up late at night and called names. I don't know how much longer I can last in this job.[1]

Exhausted Resources

Burnout is a term that is bandied about freely these days. It seems that few people can define it or explain what it is. A person might reason, "I hate my job so I must be burned out."

Burnout involves exhausting certain resources. Job boredom does not exhaust resources; it suppresses them. Webster's defines *to burn out* as "to fail, wear out, or become exhausted by making excessive demands on energy, strength, or resources." In psychological studies this term has taken on a more specific meaning to describe job stress and reactions to such stress.

Burnout describes negative work-related attitudes and behaviors. One of the first indications of burnout is a negative change in one's attitude toward the job and one's outlook on life.

A major one [change] is loss of concern for the client, and a tendency to treat clients in a detached, mechanical fashion. Other changes include increasing discouragement, pessimism, and fatalism about one's work; decline in motivation, effort, and involvement in work and increasing apathy; negativism; frequent irritability and anger with clients and colleagues; preoccupation with one's own comfort and welfare on the job; tendency to rationalize failure by blaming the clients or "the system"; and resistance to change, rigidity, and loss of creativity.[2]

With the negative attitude come physical symptoms. "These include chronic fatigue; frequent colds, flu, headaches, g.i. [gastrointestinal] disturbance, and sleeplessness; excessive use of drugs; decline in self esteem; and marital and family conflict."[3]

Burnout is not to be confused with fatigue, because burnout also involves a negative attitude. However, such an attitude can produce great fatigue. Likewise, job turnover is not always a result of burnout. Although some burnout victims do change jobs, many such people remain on the job, risking the mental and physical consequences. Many burnout victims wish they could quit their stress-related jobs, but for the sake of fear of failure, security, or loyalty to loved ones, they remain as bitter herbs in the lives of others.

What is the temperament of the professional who is prone to burnout? "Herbert Freudenberger, a psychoanalyst, who was the first to use the term burn-out in an article, argues that the dedicated and committed are most prone to burn-out. Also, those who have a strong desire to be accepted and liked by their clients are particularly susceptible."[4] *Professionals with the highest risk of burnout are those who work in helping services, who don't resolve frustrations and conflicts, and who are extremely dedicated and committed.*

After nineteen years in his profession, an Indianapolis high school principal quit his job and entered an entirely different line of work. He said, "You've got to be superhuman to take that kind of stress . . . it's not fair. Most of the teachers come from a background where they're not used to the kind of stress they encounter." When asked why he left his career, he said, "I feel I could have taken it. I just wasn't willing. I could not do the job I wanted to do." When asked if he would ever go back, he said, "You couldn't pay me a million dollars to go back."[5]

One attorney, who founded an association which serves as a retreat and treatment center for burned out lawyers, was himself a victim. At the time of his burnout he simply could not read another legal paper. He felt immensely powerless and frustrated. He was thinking of seeking a larger and more stressful ("challenging") law practice until he began treating his family as though they were on trial. He was argumentative to the point of constantly cross-examining his wife and children. When he realized what he was doing to his family and himself, he gave up his law practice and started an association to help others to recover from burnout.

In my interviews I found that women are even more vulnerable to burnout than are men. The woman who seeks a career in the corporate world or in another male-dominated type work usually finds isolation and supercompetitiveness a part of the job. She often is excluded from male social gatherings at work, and she must always prove that she can work as well or better than a man. She must also walk a psychological tightrope concerning her behavior. Her clothes must be just right; they must not give a message of sloppiness or one of sexual overtones. Her smile must be friendly but not inviting. She does not want others to think of her as a promiscuous woman. She must be careful when exercising her authority. If she is too stern, the male employees will resent her and will not work well. If she is too yielding, the men will not listen to her and will consider her weak.

A nurse who practiced for seven years in a large city experienced a change in her values as she burned out. After working in both public and private hospitals for only four years, she began feeling depressed about the profession she had thought would give her enough satisfaction to last a lifetime.

She was furious with doctors. She felt as if she had no decision-making power and was able to grow less and less each week. During her last three years as a nurse, she became hostile toward her profession and the people associated with it—doctors and patients alike. She reached the point where she was tired of giving. She was so in need of care herself, she started feeling as if she were the patient. Yet there was no one at the hospital to care for her. She left the nursing profession for a job in marketing.

Does Anybody Care?

The question, "Does anybody *really* care about me?" goes through the mind of every victim of burnout. Those who give so much of their knowledge, training, wisdom, and skills, often wonder if other people are concerned at all with how they feel.

John Byers, a middle-aged minister of a rural church, was burning out. His church was small, but its problems were great. He seemed always to be busy mediating some squabble or difficulty between church members. Many members had chronic illnesses, including his own wife, Thelma. She had heart blockage and was limited in how much she could assist her husband in his pastoral duties.

John faced many discouragements in his ministry. He walked in the footsteps of a deceased pastor whom the people always kept alive in their conversations. John's dreams of building a mighty church were crumbling day by day. Five years had passed, and there were still the same number of empty pews as there had been in his first year.

The apathy of the church members overwhelmed his zeal and enthusiasm. He lost his excitement with the ministry. It soon became merely a job. He did the more pleasant tasks and left the unpleasant ones undone. John soon began to blame the undone tasks on the pathetic church members. "If they would only do some work around here, this church would grow," he would say.

Then one night very late, the ministry of John Byers gasped its dying breath. Thelma began having difficulty breathing. He stabilized her with oxygen and medication as he had done many other times. He worried as she gasped for air and held her chest. Soon the medication and oxygen began to take effect. The one-hour ordeal was over and she was resting. It was 3:00 A.M., and John thought he might be able to get some rest before sunrise.

Just then the telephone rang. *Who could it be at this*

hour? he thought. When he heard the voice on the phone, he thought bitterly, *Oh no! Her again!* A widow in the church, a woman who had been suffering from severe depression since she lost her husband a month earlier, whined, "I have been so depressed tonight. I believe I would be better off if I could die and be with my husband. I just want you to know why I'm going to commit suicide."

John sat on the edge of the bed, looking at his ailing wife, then looking at the telephone. *What shall I do? Shall I leave my sick wife to go to the aid of this woman?* John did go to the widow's aid and counseled her for two hours. When he returned home, his wife was having another attack. This time the oxygen and medication failed to help. He called an ambulance and had her taken to the hospital. Thelma underwent open heart surgery a few hours later. Her life was in jeopardy.

John could feel guilt crushing him like a weight. He felt as guilty for leaving her alone that night as if he had committed adultery with the depressed widow. As he sat alone in the waiting room, he thought, *Who cares anything about us, anyway? If the wife of one of our deacons were sick, I would be right at her side. The only person who cares for me is in that operating room. I've given and given until I cannot help another troubled person. I need help, but there isn't any to be found.*

Thelma survived the surgery, but John did not survive in the ministry. His ministry died in that hospital waiting room. He honestly believed that no one cared. Not even God. John had weathered difficult times before. But this trial was the one that ultimately burned him out.

Setting the Scene for Burnout

There are some underlying factors that can take the life-force out of a career. A career is much like a piece of freshly cut wood with sap permeating from its every cell. If that piece of wood is placed in a fire, it will burn only on the outside. The heat will not render it to ashes. If that same piece of wood has all of its life-giving sap removed by the elements of nature, then it will quickly succumb to the trial of the flames. To use the biblical metaphor, it will become ashes and later will be cast out for men to tread upon.

Factors which cause the drying out of life-giving forces are unrealistic expectations, job saturation, stifled goals, insufficient potential, low self-esteem, and failure after success, according to burnout expert Cary Cherniss.

1. *Most burnout victims have created unrealistic expectations of one sort or another.* Initially, their career was presented to them as the "dream job" by parents, friends, or counselors. It is understood that while one is preparing for that "dream job," he or she often suffers many hardships. But those hardships are considered worth it all, because that "dream job" will give happiness, security, and a sense of fulfillment.

I had a difficult time accepting that my "dream ministry" had turned into a bad dream—almost a nightmare! My frustration finally lapsed into stagnation as I realized the pervasiveness of sin in human lives, the extent of resistance to the gospel, and the countless hours that could be spent trying to help the helpless. The pastoral ministry was not anything like my dreams and expectations of it.

We will examine the matter of unrealistic expectations at length in Chapter 3.

2. *Job saturation is common among committed and dedicated professionals.* The job infiltrates every part of one's life. The person talks about the job at breakfast, works at it all day, talks about it more at the supper table, and then when his head touches the pillow for some rest, he is still trying to figure out tomorrow's problems.

Police officers, for example, have a difficult time putting their work aside, even when off duty. Although few policemen will share the grim duties of their jobs with their wives, many of them share the petty things which can become stressful. To compound self-inflicted stress, policemen experience twenty-four-hour-a-day external stress. Even when they are at home, the whole neighborhood looks upon them as guardians. If there are any complaints about a traffic ticket or a hard time received from a cop, people voice their complaints to the policeman who lives next door. Soon the fear of facing complaints begins to affect the policeman's social life.

One police officer was so disgusted with his apartment manager that he was ready to move elsewhere. The apartment manager always boasted of the "tight security" in the apartment complex and readily gave each new tenant the name and apartment number of this police officer for problems that might arise.

Doctors, lawyers, newspaper reporters, plumbers all suffer similarly. Job saturation causes alienation from those who reinforce the internal stress. Soon the reaction is to look upon people not as real human beings with needs, but as case numbers or problem codes.

3. *Stifled goals will cause some people to lose their purpose for living.* Every achiever is a dreamer or a visionary. There are treasures at the foot of rainbows. Those treasures are our dreams of success and achievement.

God has made us to be goal-oriented; otherwise we would wander aimlessly in life without a motive or will to live. We always have great difficulty choosing the right goals, but we still choose goals, right or wrong.

Sandra was a registered nurse in a major metropolitan hospital. She had been in nursing for fifteen years at the same hospital. She had a good work record and was respected as an able nurse by the doctors and staff.

The head nurse of the intensive care unit where Sandra worked was going to retire in one month. Sandra had been dreaming of this job for many years. She thought, *I am qualified and I have the seniority. I'll ask for the promotion!* Sandra spoke with the retiring head nurse and with the head of the department of nursing. They were encouraging!

Then one week before the head nurse was to retire, a new nurse appeared on the intensive care unit first shift. She was middle-aged, arrogant, overbearing, and always spoke to Sandra with an icy stare. She was the head nurse's replacement. Sandra's dreams were shattered. She tried to continue her work at the hospital, but she soon began to hate everything connected with nursing. She burned out, left nursing, went through a vocational training school, and became a telephone repairperson.

4. *Insufficient potential can lead to burnout.* During an interview with a burned out public school teacher, I asked her if she believed she had the potential to do the work. Her answer was, "I am a dummy. I was making unrealistic expectations of myself."

It takes great courage to admit that one does not have nor will ever have the potential for a certain job. Many professionals refuse to admit insufficient potential. They continue to press body and mind to the point of exhaustion, in an attempt to achieve the unachievable.

Warren Wiersbe, a noted Christian speaker and author, once said to a gathering of ministers,

> . . . Don't try to do more than what God has given you the potential to do. If a room needs a 150-watt light bulb, don't put a 60-watt bulb in the socket and expect it to do the job. God has put you where your potential can be used. Don't envy the pastor with the large congregation and believe you could do just as good a job as the pastor of the larger church.

One must be honest with oneself, lay inflated ego aside, and determine the amount of work potential one has. Some people are capable of handling long work days, much stress, and difficult situations. Others cannot survive under such circumstances. In realizing one's potential and working within it, it may be necessary to be transferred to a different area of work or even to change jobs.

5. *Low self-esteem is detrimental to all aspects of one's*

life. Low self-esteem is readily evidenced by comments such as "I'm stupid" or "Who pays any attention to me? I don't have anything worthwhile to say." Low self-esteem results in a constant put down of one's own self. People with low self-esteem are poor achievers and usually have passive attitudes toward creativity and leadership.

What causes people to have low self-esteem? There are many theories, almost all of which point back to childhood development. In a seminar Mr. Lou Nicholes, Midwest Director of Word of Life, Inc., a Christian youth ministry, once said,

> There are two powerful factors influencing children: parental control and parental support. Parental control is the ability to manage a child's behavior. Parental support is the ability to make the child feel loved. When parental support is low and parental control is high, the parents become authoritarian and produce children with a poor self image.

Parents who discipline their children with little or no love and verbally abuse them with words like "You're stupid" or "Only a dummy would do such a thing," produce offspring with a high probability of burnout due to low self-esteem. Children need to be encouraged, not put down.

6. *A sixth factor which contributes to the drying-out of the life-giving forces of one's career is failure after success.*

Janet Miles was middle-aged, happily married, and the mother of one child. She had a lovely home, comfortable surroundings, happiness, and security.

She received a call one day from the principal of the

nearby elementary school, who wanted to know if she would be interested in substitute teaching. Janet had a degree in business, not in education, and she lacked confidence in her ability to take on the task. She told the principal that she would "think about it." After several weeks of weighing the pros and cons, she decided to take the job.

Janet soon fell in love with the challenge of teaching. "It was exciting at first. I looked forward to each day with the expectation of new and different things happening," she said.

She then decided to go back to college for her degree in education. Her drive to achieve was so strong that she proceeded to earn her Master's degree. Now she not only possessed a love for education, but she felt she was more than well qualified to do the task.

Her first assignment was to teach sixth graders. Her feelings of success as a substitute teacher soon grew dim as she faced the problems of a full-time educator. The excitement and variety were gone. Teaching was no longer something she wanted to do, but something she had to do. The family had geared its standard of living around the two-paycheck income.

After two years, she changed from a sixth grade class to second graders. *This will be better*, she thought. Though the switch was an improvement, things were never as good as when she was substitute teaching. She found herself making comments like "I'm a dummy" and "I don't have what it takes to teach."

A new principal brought about some changes which caused additional stress, including station teaching and too many field trips. The stress added to her failure complex and started Janet on the road to burnout. She began to suffer from exhaustion as early as the second hour of classtime. Migraine headaches would follow as she pushed herself to complete the day. When she came home, she fell into bed and stayed there until the next morning, neglecting her husband and daughter.

The cycle of exhaustion, headaches, and indifference left Janet in a severely depressed condition. She tolerated the physical and mental nightmare for a year. Her husband and her daughter, now seventeen, did not understand what was happening to her. They only knew she was unbearable to live with.

Janet's husband himself was lonely, dejected, and fed up with his occupation as a high school teacher. Janet came to believe he had caught burnout from her. (Cary Cherniss has discovered that burnout is contagious, especially among married couples.[7]) Then he met a young and pretty student teacher at the school where he worked. They were physically attracted to each other and he asked for a divorce, which was finalized during the darkest days of Janet's burnout.

Then Janet's daughter left home and moved to a man's apartment to live with him out of wedlock. Janet was so ashamed that she could hardly face anybody at school or in the community. Her whole world was coming apart. She thought, *Am I going insane? Do I have some disease that is doing this to me?*

Janet sought medical help. Two different doctors told her that it was all from the onset of menopause, yet she knew that menopause was not the whole problem. Other teaching colleagues had experienced menopause without such extreme mental and physical problems. They sailed right through it, while she sank like a rock.

Out of a sense of loyalty and longing for security, Janet endured teaching for three more years to earn that desperately needed paycheck. One day she knew, after a doctor's consultation, that she would have to change jobs in order to maintain her sanity. She quit with fifteen years of teaching experience, yet she considered only two of those fifteen years successful.

Janet now works as a librarian in the same town where she taught school. When she is not working, she sits alone by the fireplace in a rocker, gazing at the dried-out wood being consumed in the fire. How similar the activity in that fireplace is to her life. The flames are in complete control, as they consume that which once had so much life. Janet's life is also in ashes. Her concerns are when to take her next antidepressant pill and when her next doctor's appointment will be.

Until the time that I interviewed Janet Miles, she was unaware of a pattern in her experiences. She was not familiar with the word *burnout*. One thing she did know: Her family and career had been reduced to ashes.

7. *Lack of personal support is a final factor in why people succumb to burnout.* A Christian friend was for some

years a key administrator at a large Midwestern University. He reported to the vice-president who had hired him for the post.

After a time, his productivity expanded, the department grew impressively, and he was given the nod to hire a new assistant. After interviewing several people, he selected a thirty-year-old alumnus for the job. Things worked well at first, but after a year or so the new man began to be insubordinate. To complicate matters, the vice-president left to take the presidency of a college elsewhere.

The new vice-president agreed the assistant was conducting himself with impropriety but refused to grant the director of the department the authority to dismiss him. When the showdown finally came, there was no personal support from above. Eventually, the director sought a new position. (Ironically, a short time later, the assistant was demoted and to this day remains an also-ran in the structure of the school.)

All of us need personal support, people to check us where we err and to encourage us when we succeed. How much more valuable these support people become in times of tension. The pastor of a congregationally governed church can face special problems here if there is no strong group of elders: He has no superior. An orthodox priest looks to his bishop, the Presbyterian pastor to his district superintendent, but the Baptist or Bible Church minister often stands alone. In a congregation of two hundred, he has two hundred people to whom he reports. This is why, I believe, more and more independent church pastors are looking to pastors in neighboring churches for support. Without it, a crash landing is often imminent.

Checking the Signs

These seven factors, collectively or individually, can result in the drying out of love of, zeal for, enthusiasm and interest in a career. When combined with unresolved stress, the result is burnout. Most burnout victims have no idea why they are acting as they are until damage, physically and mentally, is done.

Certain signs or signals indicate the presence or possibility of burnout. I have found that "yes" answers to these questions are given by people who are burning out.

A. **Are you weary with your work?**
   Does it drain you emotionally?
   Do you dislike waking up in the morning because you have to go to your job again?
   Does your job frustrate you?
   Do you constantly feel at your wit's end at work?
   Do you ever think about death as a way of escape?
B. **Are you callous toward other people?**
   Do you think of the people with whom you work as objects?
   Do you notice a definite hardening of your attitude toward your fellow workers?
   Do you rejoice to see a colleague endure a hardship, especially if that person has caused you stress?
   Do you blame others for your problems and failures?

C. Are your dreams gone?
Do you blame others for hindering your success?
Have you stopped making plans to do great things?
Do you consider your career a treadmill?
Do you consider life to be one big disappointment?

D. Are you a loner?
Do you find yourself avoiding people who make your life stressful?
Do you feel as if other people, especially your supervisors, have taken something of great value from you?
Do you constantly blame others for your problems?
Do you want to be "left alone"?

If your answers are "yes" to the majority of these questions, it could be that you are entering into—or already experiencing—burnout.
Don't despair! Help is to be found.

Notes

1. Harry Levinson, "When Executives Burn Out," *Harvard Business Review*, May-June, 1981, p. 74.
2. Cary Cherniss, "Recent Research and Theory on Job Stress and Burnout in Helping Professions," Seminar

paper presented at the University of Michigan, May 12, 1978, p. 6. Used by permission.
3. Ibid.
4. Ibid., p. 8.
5. Mary Wade Atteberry, "Teacher Burnout Stalking Indiana Classrooms," *Indianapolis Star*, September 21, 1980, Section 2, p. 1.
6. Cherniss, p. 9.
7. Ibid., p. 16.

3

Most Likely to Succeed

When Barbara Doyle was a small child, her dream was to be a school teacher. While other children admired doctors, police officers, firemen, and nurses, Barbara adored her first grade teacher, Miss Bradshaw. Whenever someone asked Barbara what she wanted to be when she grew up, her answer was always, "A teacher, just like Miss Bradshaw."

As she grew older Barbara was close to all of her teachers, except the grouchy ones. She was convinced that teachers had particularly rewarding jobs, and she felt that none of them should ever have any dislike for children.

Throughout Barbara's years of schooling, she continued to believe that teaching children was the most perfect profession one could ever have. Even as she received her degree from college, she looked upon professors as symbols of intellect, achievement, self-discipline, integrity, and, most of all, success.

Her first day as a teacher finally arrived. As she entered the Jefferson Middle School, she was so scared her legs were weak. The excitement of her dreams coming true was almost more than she could bear. She was going to be able to impart knowledge to these eighth grade children. Her classroom would be her own little world in which she would be in command. The students would appreciate what she had to offer. The faculty would work together as a family in the education business. It was going to be great!

Barbara's first day was a disaster. By no special design, it just happened that she was given the third level English class to teach, which was composed of "difficult" students. She considered the assignment a challenge but found it to be a curse. The room was packed with thirty-seven students. Most of them were disheveled in appearance, reeked from lack of personal hygiene, and were arrogant in disposition. Very few had pencils or paper. They were more interested in shooting paper wads than learning about dangling participles.

After fifty long and tension-filled minutes the bell rang—the best sound she had heard all day. She rushed to the principal's office and soon broke into tears. "How can I teach these children when they won't listen?" she asked. The principal assured her that things would get better. Comforted and reinspired, she finished the day and went home believing the situation would change in the days ahead.

Days passed into weeks and weeks into months, but things were no better at all. The students were unruly. Once she sent the worst troublemaker to the principal's office. Within fifteen minutes he returned with an arrogant smirk. Soon a messenger brought a note instructing *her* to report to the principal's office after class. When he delivered a lecture about wasting his time, she realized her authority in the classroom was dissolving.

Grading papers took hours every evening. Barbara found herself sinking in a sea of exams, evaluation papers, performance records for district, state, and national administrators, gradecards, and skill profiles. "Did Miss Bradshaw have to do all this?" she asked herself. "She always seemed so composed and looked as if she enjoyed her work. Look at me! I'm coming apart at the seams!"

Barbara soon dreaded facing her students. She utilized student teachers as much as possible. More and more often, she called in sick. Barbara was so disillusioned with her dream career that she began to hate it. Any mention of the word *teacher* caused bitterness to swell up inside her. She knew something was seriously wrong when a television show about teachers came on one night. She turned it off so violently she broke the knob off the set.

Barbara resigned as a teacher after seven months in her "dream career." She later obtained a job as a librarian.

Professional Mystique

Barbara is a classic case of what psychologists have termed *professional mystique:* patterning one's life after another person or a certain image of a profession, and later becoming disillusioned with that person and/or profession. Barbara, of course, had patterned herself after Miss Bradshaw, her first grade teacher. Barbara had a mental picture during her years before teaching of what a great honor it would be to be like Miss Bradshaw. When reality didn't measure up to her fantasy, Barbara's world came crashing in on her.

Professional mystique is not unique to teachers. Business executives, physicians, attorneys, ministers, and especially social workers are drawn in by this illusion. None are exempt.

Where does professional mystique start? How far back do we need to search in order to find the primary cause for such patterning?

Small children admire heroes. Some heroes are able to leap over tall buildings with a single bound and fly faster than a speeding bullet. Children love these heroes, but soon understand that they are fantasy. But other heroes, such as nurses, police officers, doctors, and teachers, are more down to earth. So why shouldn't the ideal be true?

For example, many times in my years in the pastorate, I had small children tell me they wanted to be a preacher like me. Sometimes they even pretended to be preacher and congregation in their playtime. They dreamed about the popularity, the prestige, and the independent lifestyle a minister supposedly has.

As children grow older, the image of the particular hero is reinforced by friends who have the same illusion and by family members who desire the prestige of a professional in the family. Pressure especially comes to bear from family members who are not professionals. Many dads have said to their sons, "I break my back and work my fingers to the bone for a living. I want you to get a good education. Then you can be the boss, make lots of money, and be happy at your work." Professional mystique often has its beginnings, then, in the dreams of others. Such dreams lack the information that is vital for career decision making. The "dream career" based on faulty information is a straw man quickly consumed by the fiery trials of professional reality.

The Perfect Job

One study of professional mystique, conducted by a team of psychologists from the University of Michigan, concluded professional mystique perpetuates illusions in six areas. They include job autonomy, belief that the job will be challenging, equating credentials with competence, belief that colleagues will have unity, belief that clients will be grateful, and the belief that professionals have all the answers.

1. *The primary lure to a profession is job autonomy: possessing the ability to control one's own work environment.* Being a professional businessman, teacher, lawyer, physician, or social worker supposedly means freedom and control over decisions affecting one's work.

But a study of professional and nonprofessional civil service workers discovered blue-collar workers engaged in maintenance work had more autonomy than professionals. The trend in professional circles is, the bigger the bureaucracy the more limited the autonomy. This lack of control and sense of powerlessness leads to disillusionment concerning the job and eventually to burnout.[1]

2. *The second element in professional mystique is a belief that the dream career will be interesting, challenging, have plenty of variety, and most of all, be fulfilling.* Most young professionals find out quickly that intrinsically their careers are anything but interesting, challenging, varied, or fulfilling.

A study of lawyers working in neighborhood legal aid offices revealed that most of the lawyers felt their work was too narrow and confining.

> Much to the surprise of many new legal aid lawyers, the intellectual and legal issues in these cases are usually clear cut and thus uninteresting; and even when they occasionally are not, the legal aid attorney has neither the time nor the mandate to think through and work on the more intricate and interesting issues. Over time, much of the interest and challenge simply disappears; what began as a "calling" increasingly becomes simply a job.[2]

Teachers experience this disillusionment also. Some teachers spend years in higher education and thousands of dollars in order to be effective. As in the opening illustration to the chapter, they see the glamor of being loved by their students—not the hours grading papers, the uncooperative parents and administration, the discipline problems, and the low pay. Their hands tied, many succumb to simply being "babysitters" or giving their students busy work.

3. *The third element of professional mystique is equating credentials with competence.* The notion is widespread that a college or graduate degree is proof that a person is "able." Most professionals admit that the beginning of a career is shocking.

A public health nurse drove around the block three times on her way to her first interview before she finally mustered the courage to knock on the patient's door. A new lawyer confessed that initially he had no idea of how one makes motions in court or files papers for clients; and until he "learned the ropes," he was constantly afraid of mistakes and appearing inept.[3]

Of course, employers expect a certain amount of mistakes from new employees. But employers usually are more tolerant of blue-collar mistakes than errors made by so-called professionals. A blue-collar worker might destroy a ten-thousand-dollar piece of equipment, but be forgiven on the basis of "beginner's error." If a college-trained professional makes such a costly mistake in his first week on the job, it probably will result in a black mark on his work record. Why? Because credentials are equated with competence, by employers and professional employees.

4. *The fourth element of professional mystique is the belief that colleagues will have unity.* This expectation could possibly be a carryover from college and graduate school days. Institutions of higher education usually are the scene of a strong spirit of comraderie. The purposes, aims, and lifestyles of the students are very similiar. But that *esprit de corps* disappears on graduation day, never to reappear. Even alumni gatherings are rife with one-upmanship.

The professional often leads an isolated life at work. The higher one goes in the corporate structure, the lonelier it becomes. Many professionals agree that their contacts with fellow colleagues are rare. Contacts that are made are often characterized by undercutting, rivalry, competition, and distrust—a situation that is hardly conducive for any type of fellowship.[4]

This loneliness can be devastating to a young professional, especially to one who was active in college projects that involved close work with colleagues. The unexpected change produces a homesickness for "the good old days," when people cared for each other. An unstable home life or marital problems will only make the situation worse. The young professional soon believes that nobody cares and that there is no place to retreat.

5. *The fifth element of professional mystique is the shock of having ungrateful clients.* The professional new to the field believes that every client will be grateful and honest in all dealings. It is reasonable to believe that if you treat the one you are helping with honesty, integrity, and love, then you will be treated with honesty, integrity, and love in return. But that is not the way things happen in the real world!

A study of patient compliance in medical practice suggests that at least one-third of all patients fail to follow the physician's advice. New poverty lawyers were shocked to learn that their clients frequently lied to them. The clients felt that their lawyers were a part of the system which manipulated them. Interviews with new high school teachers revealed that they were frequently "chumped" or "had" by students who took advantage of the teacher's trust or permissiveness.[5]

Cary Cherniss speaks of this helpless feeling. "When the lack of resources and power is chronic a phenomenon called 'learned helplessness' develops. The individual just concludes there's nothing he or she can do to make things better and gives up trying."[6]

6. *The sixth element of professional mystique is the belief that professionals have all the answers to life's problems.* This idea is based on presumption that education imparts wisdom. If the young doctor has a medical degree in hand, he certainly should be able to solve almost every problem—from any field—which confronts him.

The entertainment business has created much of the image that educated professionals are filled with great wisdom. Television's problem solvers not only succeed at their duties as professionals but also go beyond the call of duty to give expert advice, show compassion, and sacrifice time and money to help those who have special needs. We have seen the wisdom of *Marcus Welby, M.D.*, the concern of *White Shadow* for his basketball players, and the personal interest of *Quincy*, as these professionals solve crises in sixty minutes. The young professional quickly concludes, after giving some erroneous counseling which backfires, that he must be inferior or else he would have the answers.

These six elements compose professional mystique. All six elements contain the seeds of disillusionment. Disillusionment is usually the product of faulty information, wrong values, and misguided motives. When the disillusioned person meets up with the reality of having built a career on faulty information, wrong values, and misguided motives, his or her dreams shatter. This extreme disappointment and discouragement can eventually lead to burnout.

"My Son Is in Christian Work"

Professional mystique was very much a part of my own childhood. I was reared in a family known for its ministers. Whenever our family gathered for reunions, the pastors were always the center of attention. They led in prayer, told witty stories, made everyone laugh, initiated the games, and closed the day with a challenge from God's Word.

I held these ministers in incredibly high esteem. They seemed to enjoy life and to love their work. They had the admiration of everybody. But these ministers were not in my immediate family, except for my grandfather who lived two hundred miles from me. I never had the chance to be with them in day-to-day living.

My dad was not a minister but a salesman. I saw the realities of that occupation through him. The trials and ordeals he endured painted a true picture for me as to the life of a salesman.

Two years after I accepted Jesus Christ as my Savior, I experienced a burden for others and a desire to preach the gospel. While this decision was never directly influenced by my minister relatives, I must say I was glad God had brought me into that select group of my family. I had much honor bestowed upon me as I completed my seminary training and accepted my first pastorate. I was the leader at family gatherings.

I must confess that I had to deal with the sin of pride as a young minister. Pride easily creeps in when you keep hearing your parents say, "This is our son, the seminary graduate and minister." All the time I was thinking, *Being in the ministry is really great! Now I know why my grandfather, uncles, and cousins always seemed so happy at family gatherings. People really admire and appreciate ministers!*

After a few years in the ministry, I learned the other side of that career, which my relatives had not had opportunity to let me in on. Perhaps they hid their frustrations, stresses, disappointments, and discouragements from the people around them, for I learned to do the same. Let me hasten to add that I am certain I, at one time or another, was guilty of establishing the professional mystique in the heart of some young person.

The harsh realities of the ministry almost made me think my relatives had lied to me. It was as though they had lied by not sharing with me the whole picture, even when they knew I was entering that profession. Professional mystique was certainly an element leading to my own burnout. How responsible was I for my own naivete, and could my disappointment have been avoided by some concerned minister giving me the whole picture? My ignorance was not bliss.

Notes

1. Cary Cherniss, Edward S. Egnatios, Sally Wacker, Bill O'Dowd, "The Professional Mystique and Burnout in Public Sector Professionals," Seminar paper presented at the University of Michigan, p. 6. Used by permission.
2. Ibid., p. 8.
3. Ibid.
4. Ibid., p. 9.
5. Ibid., p. 10.
6. Cary Cherniss, "Recent Research and Theory on Job Stress and Burnout in Helping Professions," Seminar paper presented at the University of Michigan, May 12, 1978, p. 12.

4

In the Bind

For many years the word *stress* was used primarily by architects and engineers. The term was used in reference to bridges, buildings, highways, and other projects, which had to endure heavy weights and pressures.

Then *stress* was adopted to describe psychological or physical strain on human beings. Before long people were talking about stress as if it were a newly discovered, dreaded disease. The goal of workers was to escape it. People dreamed of the stress-free life. Stories spread like wildfire of those who had quit the rat race and left a pressure-cooker career to make ceramic pots in the desert. "Oh, to be free from the pressures of this job" is still the cry of hundreds of thousands of men and women workers under daily stress. This type of thinking is built on the premise that all stress is bad and should be avoided.

Contrary to the dreams of many, a life with no stress at all would be very boring. Gary Collins, professor of pastoral psychology at Trinity Evangelical Divinity School, says, "Studies have found that too little stimulation, a life devoid of challenges or changes, can produce many of the same physiological symptoms and disorders as overwork."[1]

Stress may come from surrounding circumstances or from within the individual. Stress also may be mild, moderate, or severe, depending upon the amount, type of stress, and the physical and psychological strength of the person. *Positive stress* is that influence or stimulus which causes the individual to be motivated and compete for better quality work and general productivity in life. *Negative stress* is that influence or stimulus which becomes harmful to the worker. Work activity is hindered because of the mental and physical problems it produces.

Three Categories of Stress

There seems to be a definite relationship between negative, undealt-with stress and burnout. Stress is only the flexing of emotional resources; in burnout those resources are utterly depleted. The depletion, of course, is brought on by constant and unresolved stress. Collins, in his book *Man in Transition*, divides stresses into three categories: those which arise from frustration, those resulting from conflicts, and those which come from pressures.[2]

1. *There are frustrations.* Every human being experiences frustration in life. Frustration is the feeling that occurs when an obstacle prevents a person from reaching a goal. When a toddler cannot reach her toy, frustration occurs. When a senior citizen doesn't receive his Social Security check on time to pay the rent,

he is frustrated. No one is exempt from external frustrations, such as a flat tire on the freeway, or internal frustrations, such as a desire for a position that cannot be reached.

2. *There are conflicts.* A conflict is decision making between two or more goals. Ironically, people often take vacations to get away from decision making; but vacations, themselves, are usually loaded with conflicts. Where shall we stay? Where shall we eat? Whom shall we visit? How shall we pay for it all? Conflicts are all around us—at work, at home, and at play. Three types of conflicts are encountered almost daily.

The *I like both goals* conflict arises when a person must choose a single goal between two favorable ones. The corporate executive who likes his present job and is offered a better job faces this type of conflict.

There is also the *I dislike both results* conflict. In this conflict the person desires neither of the results. A person in great pain with a toothache, who detests dentists experiences this type of conflict.

The *I like the goal but dislike some of the results* is the most common conflict. A supervisor of a major manufacturing firm was offered a position in middle management. He had always dreamed of having that position. But then he learned the job was available because the former executive had burned out under the pressures. This type of conflict is a source of stress, because it leads to great vacillation and indecision.

3. *There are pressures.* Pressures are demands that tend to squeeze a person into certain behavior pat-

terns. These can be external, as in the case of a sales-man whose manager demands that he achieve a certain quota or he will be fired. They can also be internal, as in the case of a new manager who believes he will never achieve greater results than his predecessor.

Not uncommonly all three types of stress converge upon a person in a single day. If negative stress is dealt with quickly, then the damage is minimal. If negative stress is prolonged by avoidance or denial, then the damage to the person—both mentally and physically—is more severe. John T. Biggs, a St. Louis psychiatrist, points out: "Most people deny that a stress problem exists until they produce a series of symptoms that mimic physical illness. When no physical cause can be found for dizziness, headaches, weakness, anxiety attacks, or depression, an emotional cause should seriously be considered."[3]

Stress that remains undealt with can lead to a variety of physical problems, including insomnia, sexual dysfunction, heart palpitations, indigestion, diarrhea, bronchial asthma, obesity, and pain from muscle spasms. It can also lead to such behavior problems as hostile aggressiveness, impatience, restlessness, explosive temper and speech, sleeplessness, constant haste, excessive smoking and drinking, and infidelity.[4]

On-the-Job Stress

One of the most crucial scenes for stress is the work place. And as was said earlier, the dedicated worker often prolongs negative stress by bringing the job home. The physical results can be severe.

"In Chicago a teacher's union stress survey found 56.6% of 5,500 respondents (out of 22,000 surveyed—a 25% response) claiming physical and/or mental illness as a direct result of their jobs. While in 1962 more than one-fourth of all teachers had 20 years of experience, by 1976 this proportion had been cut in half."[5]

Pamela Bardo was a high school teacher for seventeen years in California. Due to the protection of tenure, she had one of the safest jobs in the state. "Nothing as minor as incompetence, absenteeism, laziness, or drunkenness is cause enough for dismissal in the Southern California high school where I taught," she wrote.[6]

Yet, with all this job security, Pamela quit her teaching profession and became a stockbroker. What was it that she could not cope with as a teacher? Pamela quit teaching because of burnout.

My complaint, however, was not that the students were behaving any worse than usual. Right up to my final day of teaching last January, my teenaged pupils arrived late, cheated on tests, forgot their supplies, fought with each other, smoked in the restrooms, sneaked out of class. I had been a teacher long enough to regard this behavior as normal. I expected teenagers to be teenagers, which means that they whisper to their classmates, make obscene gestures to kids across the room, design paper airplanes, mark on their desks, complain about homework, and distract me at every opportunity. I could handle that.

What I encountered in recent years was much more

disturbing, even frightening. In increasing numbers, teenagers have begun using their ultimate weapon against the school, the teachers, and themselves: They are simply refusing to do the work that leads to learning.

Yet, no matter how brilliant the lessons I prepared, no matter how much I personally cared for learning, no matter how expensive the tools I brought to my classroom, little learning could occur when the students didn't care to learn. Unable to learn for them, unable to sit at my desk and ignore them, I found the only solution for me was to quit teaching.[7]

Pamela attributed her burnout to the nonconcern of her students to learn. She did mention some other student behavior problems, to which she said, "I could handle that." Could she? Quite often, those who burn out do not recognize all of the frustration, conflict, and pressure stresses about them. Usually the most disturbing negative stress is determined the sole culprit.

Hans Selye is one of the world's leading authorities on stress. He has produced an inventory of stress-producing forces experienced by many teachers. There are not one, nor two, but nine various forms of stress in the life of the average teacher. These forms of stress are also applicable to most all those who have helping jobs. They are in the areas of expectations, self-fulfillment, ego needs, student-teacher relations, personal competence, self-relationship, conflicting values, social approval, and professional constraints.[8]

With such a wide array of stresses pressing down on teachers, it's a wonder there are any educators at all still on the job! Today teachers of America are heading for the endangered species list because of the numerous stress casualties which that profession has suffered.

Teachers are not the only people who work under stress. The National Institute for Occupational Safety and Health has listed the following occupations (in alphabetical order) as high stress jobs:

Administrator	Miner
Bank teller	Musician
Clergyman	Nurse's aide
Computer programmer	Office manager
Dental assistant	Painter
Electrician	Plumber
Farm owner	Policeman
Fireman	Practical nurse
Foreman	Public-relations person
Guard watchman	Railroad switchman
Hairdresser	Registered nurse
Health aide	Sales manager
Health technician	Sales representative
Inspector	Secretary
Laborer	Social worker
Lab technician	Structural-metal worker
Machinist	Teacher's aide
Machine operator	Telephone operator
Meatcutter	Waitress/Waiter
Mechanic	Warehouse worker

Test Yourself for Stress

Most all jobs create some stress, but those which deal with the public, especially helping professions, are inherently stressful. Some people who are in these high-stress occupations recognize neither the stress nor its effects until damage has resulted, either physically or mentally. Can one really tell if he has built-up negative stress? Yes! Rosalind Forbes, author of *Corporate Stress and Life Stress*, has formulated a stress test to determine what one's pressure is on the job.[9]

To take the test, read the question, mark the space which reflects your answer, total the points, and read the comments associated with your score.

	Never	Seldom	Some-times	Often	Always
1. Do you try to do as much as possible in the least amount of time?	__1	__2	__3	__4	__5
2. Are you impatient with delays, interruptions?	__1	__2	__3	__4	__5
3. Do you have to win at games to enjoy yourself?	__1	__2	__3	__4	__5
4. Are you unlikely to ask for help with a problem?	__1	__2	__3	__4	__5
5. Do you constantly strive to better your position or achievements?	__1	__2	__3	__4	__5

	Never	Seldom	Some-times	Often	Always

6. Do you constantly seek the respect and admiration of others?   __1 __2 __3 __4 __5

7. Are you overly critical of the way others do their work?   __1 __2 __3 __4 __5

8. Do you have the habit of often looking at your watch?   __1 __2 __3 __4 __5

9. Do you spread yourself too thin in terms of time?   __1 __2 __3 __4 __5

10. Do you have the habit of doing more than one thing at a time?   __1 __2 __3 __4 __5

11. Do you ever get angry or irritable?   __1 __2 __3 __4 __5

12. Do you have a tendency to talk quickly or hasten conversation?   __1 __2 __3 __4 __5

13. Do you consider yourself hard-driving?   __1 __2 __3 __4 __5

14. Do your friends or relatives consider you hard-driving?   __1 __2 __3 __4 __5

15. Do you have a tendency to get involved in multiple projects?   __1 __2 __3 __4 __5

	Never	Seldom	Some-times	Often	Always
16. Do you have a lot of deadlines in your work?	__1	__2	__3	__4	__5
17. Do you feel vaguely guilty if you relax or go out of the office at lunchtime?	__1	__2	__3	__4	__5
18. Do you take on too many responsibilities?	__1	__2	__3	__4	__5

If your score is 18 to 30, you probably work best in nonstressful, noncompetitive situations, like to set your own pace, and concentrate on one task at a time. Interruptions drive you crazy. Stress is likely to hinder your performance rather than enhance it.

If your score is 31 to 60, you can handle a bit of stress and probably enjoy it as long as it doesn't happen during more than about 20 percent of your working hours.

If your score is 61 to 90, look out! The people who work with you better look out, too. You need constant pressure in order to perform. You tend to stay up all night to finish reports or you expand tasks to increase pressure when deadlines or the job's demands aren't stressful enough. You probably grind your teeth.

If your score was in the 61 to 90 category, your situation is dangerous if not handled properly. The human body and mind were not designed to hold such extreme pressures. Something has to give.

Burn Out or Rust Out

Mark Turner was a young missionary who experienced the results of the destructive forces of stress: burnout. He had been taught as a youth that a missionary was to be dedicated and willing to sacrifice "everything" for the cause of Christ. He interpreted "sacrifice" to mean even his physical and emotional health. His college training further enforced this interpretation with a popular saying among missionaries, "I'd rather burn out than rust out."

When Mark and his family arrived in a large South American city, he was ready to evangelize its three million inhabitants. His first goal was to place Christian literature into one hundred thousand homes the first year on the field. His second goal was to start a self-supporting church. His third goal was to train a national pastor for that church before his four-year term expired. He achieved all those goals.

Four years later Mark arrived back in the United States for a one-year furlough. He weighed forty-five pounds less than when he went; he was suffering from exhaustion, depression, and many physical ailments.

After furlough, Mark and his family returned to the same mission field and to the work which he had established. His physical and emotional state was still shaky, yet his goals were just as high as before.

Soon the stress started again. Only half the money had been raised for the church building program. There were discipline problems in the church which caused division. Then came more work when he was given teaching duties in a newly formed Bible institute.

Soon things began to come unraveled. The work became a vicious cycle, going faster and faster. All he could think about was getting off that spinning carousel of stress. He tried to find relief by avoiding the stressful situations, but he quickly found them inescapable. Finally it happened. Mark suffered a complete burnout and emotional breakdown. He had to be brought back to the United States for rest and emotional therapy. Mark Turner did indeed burn out rather than rust out.

How could Mark Turner have prevented the negative stress which led to his burnout? What can the hundreds of thousands of workers who are faced with negative stress do to make certain that they do not experience the trauma of burnout?

There is a system for the relief of external and internal stresses. Some of the factors within this system are temporal, while others are more lasting. The system is composed of physical and mental elements, which must be developed just as one would build up a muscle.

Relief in Action

As you may have already surmised from our overview in the previous chapters, stress is basically a problem of the mind. Hans Selye suggests seven mental actions which can be practiced by the individual to relieve stress. They are setting realistic expectations, establishing priorities, enjoying meditation, learning to laugh again, living today's life, being thankful, and recognizing the differences in stresses.

1. *The first mental action is to set realistic expectations.* Most professional workers do not have realistic expectations but are idealistic, setting their short- and long-range goals at impossible heights. Setting such high goals is supposed to cause individuals to do more than their best. But the results fall far short.

Constantly failing to achieve goals results in an emotional behavior called *shifting unachievable goals.* "Some of the main symptoms of this chronic emotional illness are: (i) general disregard and disdain for one's achievements, however worthy these may be, (ii) a sense of "falling short" and "just missing the mark," (iii) a feeling of bitterness and ingratitude."[10] Those who set unachievable goals at work will more than likely do so in other areas also, such as in family and social relations. Failing to achieve unrealistic goals at the office will cause the stressed person to shift even more unrealistic goals upon one's family or friends to compensate.

There is a theological matter which I want to mention relative to proper expectations. We seem to be living in a "Victory in Jesus" era, where much evangelical preaching and teaching stresses only the joy and glory of the faith. Thankfully, there is infinite joy and glory which is ours in Christ. But what about sermons on the setbacks, disappointments, and persecutions that faced God's people in Scripture?

If the expectations in Christ are perpetual victory, positive thinking, and pristine glee, one has captured but half the gospel of the kingdom. As someone has suggested, we need to go back and read the verses we *didn't* underline. The road to Christian victory is paved with costly struggle and perseverance.

Goals must be challenging, otherwise they would be meaningless. But goals must be set within reach—not like the brass ring on a carousel ride.

2. *Relieving stress also involves the establishment of right priorities.* Professional workers live in constant tension between the urgent and the important. Usually the important tasks are laid aside because of the urgent ones. The invention of the "electronic ball and chain," the telephone beeper, has made us slaves of the urgent. How can we establish a way of knowing what is urgent and what is important?

Evaluate the situation. Write down all your commitments. Include in this list all commitments at work, home, church, and community. Then number the commitments according to your responsibility to them.

Then, *ask God's guidance.* God is one who respects order. His handiwork in creation is proof that He does things in an orderly fashion. Pray over the list. Ask God to give you guidance and help make you sensitive to *His* order.

Finally, *stick to those priorities.* Learn to say no to the demands of the urgent, which try to distort your priorities. Say no with love, but stick to your list of priorities. Yet don't consider your list of priorities as a straightjacket, as some undisciplined people do. Instead, look upon your list of priorities as a track to guide you and to keep you from having a stress wreck.

3. *Enjoying meditation will relieve stress.* The belief is common that one must be a far Eastern mystic in order to enjoy meditation. This is not so. The Bible, God's Word to all people, says, "Blessed is the man that walketh not in the counsel of the ungodly, nor standeth in the way of sinners, nor sitteth in the seat of the scornful. But his delight is in the law of the LORD; and in his law doth he *meditate* day and night" (Ps. 1:1,2, italics mine).

Meditation is sole concentration on one positive thing. Worry is the flip side of meditation. If one wishes to empty a container of harmful materials that cannot be dumped, how can it be emptied? Fill the container with that which is good. Then, the bad flows out and is replaced fully by the good. What is your first thought when your eyes open in the morning?

Many stress-filled people start out their day with the thought, "Oh no, it's morning. Another day at that job." The mind is filled immediately with negative thoughts. The Bible says, "Whatsoever things are true, whatsoever things are honest, whatsoever things are just, whatsoever things are pure, whatsoever things are lovely, whatsoever things are of good report; if there be any virtue, and if there be any praise, think [meditate, concentrate] on these things" (Phil. 4:8). God tells us to focus on that which is good and godly—especially the promises to the children of God.

I find it a comfort to meditate on these promises during difficult days. One time, while reading Romans 8:28, "And we know that all things work together for good to them that love God, to them who are the called according to his purpose," I was perplexed about the word "good" in this promise. The trials and tribulations which I had been enduring did not seem good at all. Then I began to meditate on the subject of "good." God opened my understanding of good. God's good is much broader in scope than we realize. His eternal purpose allows both evil and good to work toward our good. My finite vantage point limited my overall perspective of God's purpose.

The obedient Christian seeks to occupy his or her mind with the good things of God. Meditate upon the good things which God has given. This meditation will give a breath of fresh air to a mind that has been filled with the smog of stress.

4. *Learning to laugh again will alleviate stress considerably.* Built-up negative stress will turn a smile into a frown. The entire nation has seen the effects of stress upon the faces of our presidents. When they campaigned and as they assumed the Oval Office, the presidential candidates had radiant smiles. But after several years, under the constant stress of the problems of the presidency, those radiant smiles turn into hard, set frowns. Stress can be internalized, but it can't be hidden for long.

Comedians have known for years that laughter is a temporary relief for stress. This is why adults enjoy the antics of a clown as much as children do. Laughter is a quick release for a stressful situation. There is always a humorous side to any stressful encounter. Look for it and laugh at it. Maybe it can only be a chuckle on the inside, but it certainly beats crying on the inside.

5. *To cope with stress one must learn to live today's life.* Don't worry about tomorrow. Worrying about future board evaluations, deadlines, and promotions make

for undue stress. Worrying about tomorrow is like saying, "I don't have enough stress today, so I believe I will borrow some of tomorrow's problems."

For many years I was a strong advocate of living by a weekly priority list. I would write a list of my priorities for the week, the order in which they were to be done, and the times of the day these duties would be carried out. I soon became a slave to that list. Whenever an emergency interrupted my schedule I felt that interruption had wrecked the order in my life. I constantly felt backlogged with duties to do and no time to do them. I began to worry about those undone duties and felt pressured by them constantly. I grew to hate that list but believed I could not work without it. One day I threw my time schedule into the wastebasket. I made a new list with only the priorities on it (see suggestion number 2 above). I refuse to put a time limit on my life again. If God interrupts my priorities with something outside my routine, I believe He is showing me where the real priorities are.

Jesus Christ knew that negative stress was harmful, for He said, "Therefore do not be anxious about tomorrow, for tomorrow will be anxious for itself. Let the day's own trouble be sufficient for the day," (Matt. 6:34 RSV). Take one day at a time. Don't even worry about the things of the present day. Worrying comes from having an attitude that everything is out of control and that there is nothing anybody can do to help it. Such an attitude is rebuked many times by God in His Word (see 1 Pet. 5:7; Matt. 6:25–34).

6. *A crucial action in alleviating stress concerns being thankful.* Ingratitude is the result of built-up negative stress and is prominent in burnout. Seeing the good

things in a job is difficult, because bitterness and frustrations make the bad things seem so large. Many business executives have burned out of a career that had good pay, excellent benefits, hard-working staff, and other positive things. But because of a negative, stress-producing element, the situation seemed impossible. Ingratitude will always make one believe that the "whole" job is unbearable, because one part is.

Thankfulness is the product of a heart that is right with God. When one realizes that every good and perfect gift comes from God (see James 1:17), and that even stressful situations can be used of God for the good of the believer (see 1 Pet. 1:6,7), then there can be thankfulness in every situation. Philippians 4:6 says, ". . . in every thing by prayer and supplication *with thanksgiving* let your requests be made known unto God" (italics mine).

7. *The seventh mental action is recognizing the differences in stress.* As said earlier, not all stress is bad or negative. One should welcome and encourage constructive stress. Right amounts of it will incite penetrating thinking and task completion. "Because we think a stress is tension producing and expect it to precipitate anxiety, it usually does. But when we recognize that certain kinds of stress are normal, desirable, healthy and functional, these stresses cease to be stressful."[11]

Physical Outlet

We have talked about stress and mental attitudes. There is another element of this stress release system:

the physical outlet for stress. The mind and body are so intricately interwoven that the physical stress release must be used in coordination with the mental stress release, and vice versa. Otherwise neither will work. There are two parts to this element: *proper rest* and *the right type of exercise.*

The American "strong person" image causes many professionals not to get adequate rest. For some reason, the belief has developed that only lazy people need to sleep and get adequate rest. Thus, the successful white-collar worker is projected as one who puts in eighteen-hour days and feels great with three or four hours of sleep. Some businessmen, teachers, ministers, and other professionals even feel guilty about sleeping eight hours.

Jesus knew the importance of adequate rest after a stressful day. When his twelve disciples returned to Him after a concentrated time of preaching the gospel, healing the sick, and contending with the enemies of Christianity, Jesus took all of them into a desert place and rested a while (see Mark 6:31). Burning out from stress and physical exhaustion certainly is not God's will for any person.

Learn to relax as you rest. Just being away from the job does not always relieve stress. Thinking about the job can keep a person tense all through the night and into the next day.

One way to relieve tension is by controlled breathing. One expert has observed,

When there is an abundance of oxygen in the body, muscles tend to relax easily. Since a rapidly paced,

74

tense person usually takes short, shallow breaths, his inhalation pattern actually inhibits relaxation. Taking slow, deep breaths benefits the heart by providing a longer resting period between working beats and reducing its workload.[12]

It is best to perform deep breathing exercises on an empty stomach. Follow this procedure:

Step one: Sitting or lying down, put one hand on your stomach, the other on your chest. When you inhale, you should feel your stomach expand, then your chest. Step two: Sigh deeply, exhaling to the sound "Haaaah" three times. Step three: Inhale to the count of five, pause five, exhale five. During the inhalation, imagine bringing energy into your body. When you exhale, feel your body releasing tension and worries. To start, do about ten deep breaths, then gradually increase your number of counts during inhalation to ten; then take about twenty more breaths. Step four: Allow breathing to return to normal and focus attention on your regular breath.[13]

Warning: Do not do this breathing exercise while driving or operating machinery. The extra amounts of oxygen can cause light-headedness or dizziness.

The other part of the physical element of stress relief is *physical exercise*. Most white-collar workers get little if any physical exercise. About the only exercise that accountants, editors, lawyers, and bankers get is the walk from the parking lot to the office, which is usually less than one hundred yards.

Not all exercise will relieve stress. Sometimes a

hard game of tennis will only cause the corporate executive to be more tense. The reason: Some sports are competitive and competition produces stress!

There is a principle called "stress switching," which when practiced can help some people to change their type of stress. A steelworker faces a day filled with physical activity. He may find that the mental exercise of listening to a political speech or a sermon helps to relieve his physical stress. The teacher, who must think quickly all day, could not relieve her mental stress by getting involved in a political speech or a sermon. An aerobics dance class would help her unwind. I recommend that blue-collar workers can find "stress switching" relief by getting involved in a teaching program in a church. White-collar workers will not usually find "stress switching" relief in an academic setting but by serving their churches in a nonacademic, noninstructional way, such as singing in the choir, doing repair work, driving a bus, or heading up the softball team. Yet ironically, aren't people usually given places of service in the church to match their occupations?

It must be understood that stress switching is not true stress relief. It is a change in the type of stress. Some people consider the idea helpful; others believe it gives no relief at all.

What ways are there to release stress through noncompetitive physical activity? Walking, hiking, biking, skiing, sailing, skating, swimming—any activities that involve exercise but not competitiveness can relieve stress. Of course, any of these activities can produce stress, too, if practiced with a perfectionist attitude. Physical exercise not only tones up a flabby body but also makes sharp a dull mind. The clear mind, not clouded by the fog of inactivity, is able to set in motion a balanced, calm approach to life's problems.

A balanced combination of walking by faith and constructive exercise is a helpful antidote to the stress conditions we all face every day.

Notes

1. Gary Collins, *Man in Transition* (Carol Stream, Ill.: Creation House, 1971), p. 170.
2. Ibid., pp. 154–160.
3. June Roth, "Executive Stress: How To Help Him Relax," *Harper's Bazaar*, October, 1979, p. 175. Used by permission.
4. Ibid., p. 229.
5. Debbie Walsh, "Classroom Stress and Teacher Burnout," *Phi Delta Kappan*, December, 1979, p. 253.
6. Pamela Bardo, "The Pain of Teacher Burnout: A Case History," *Phi Delta Kappan*, December, 1979, p. 252. Used by permission.
7. Ibid.
8. Ken Styles and Gary Cavanagh, "Stress in Teaching and How to Handle It," *English Journal*, January, 1977, pp. 77,78.
9. Rosalind Forbes, *Corporate Stress and Life Stress* (Garden

City, N.Y.: Doubleday, 1979), pp. 136–138. Used by permission.
10. Styles and Cavanagh, p. 78.
11. Ibid., p. 79.
12. Roth, p. 229.
13. Forbes, pp. 76,77.

5

Emancipation From Desolation

Dr. David Hatfield knew all about guilt. It overshadowed him until he thought he would smother. He tried alcohol, drugs, consultations with a psychiatric colleague, and he even tried attending a mystical meditation group.

David knew he could not continue with his life as he was. His successful medical practice in the suburbs of Peoria was suffering because of his carelessness, loss of concern, and sarcastic attitude toward his patients. His marriage was suffering even more than his medical practice. His wife had been patient with David's many hours away from home while at work, but his use of alcohol and drugs was more than she could bear. She was suing David for divorce.

David was a burned out physician. He thought, *What does a doctor do when he burns out? Do I take an unskilled laborer's job and suffer ridicule? Must I resign to a life controlled by drugs as some of my colleagues have? Will I lose my reason completely and take my life?* David asked himself constantly, *Why me? Why has all this tragedy happened to me?*

One evening, after working many hours at the hospital, David walked through the waiting room to the entrance. His legs would hardly carry him for lack of strength. The pills didn't seem to give him much of a boost anymore. He wondered how much longer he could maintain his sanity. As he reached to open the door he saw a business card lying on the magazine table. He picked it up and read it. There was only one word: *Desperate?* Below that was a telephone number. He was compelled by something which he could not explain to dial the number. He heard the telephone ring once, twice, and three times. Just as David was ready to slam down the receiver a man with a pleasant voice said, "Hello, this is Desperation Hotline. May we help you?" David was silent. The man spoke again, "Hello, may we help you?"

With a broken voice, David said, "I have this friend who has a serious problem. He is so troubled he is even thinking of suicide. Could you help him?"

The man answered calmly, "We can certainly try. We have helped quite a few people with some serious problems."

"Who are you and what qualifies you to help people?" asked David. The man assured David that all the workers on their counseling staff were well-trained and qualified to talk to him about his problems. David made an appointment to meet with one of the counselors the next morning, all the while wondering if he would have the nerve to keep it.

When David pulled up in front of the address given to him at nine, he almost drove away. *A church! I don't need a sermon! I need help!* he raged. Again he felt the same compulsion he had experienced in the hospital waiting room. David left his car and entered the building. The structure looked like most other churches he had seen, although he had not been inside a church for twenty years. He had always insisted he could do without all that organized religion.

He heard footsteps and turned quickly to see who it was. A young man said, "Hello, I'm Bob Jarvis. You must be David Hatfield." As David shook Bob's hand he concluded that this encounter wasn't going to work out. David was in his late forties, and Bob looked to be in his early twenties. David felt he should be telling this fellow the facts of life rather than seeking counsel from him. But David couldn't seem to walk away. He was feeling that compelling power again. David was reluctant to seek Bob's guidance, but he went into the counseling room anyway.

David was hesitant to give much information right away. He only answered questions briefly. But shortly his heart became so burdened with his problems that he burst into tears and poured out the details of his wrecked life.

Bob asked, "David, do you feel guilty?"

David said, "Yes, there are some things in my life I feel great guilt about. I've tried to forget, but they keep bothering me."

"What things are bothering you?"

David looked at Bob and said, "You look as if you have had an easy life. You were probably reared in a middle class, suburban family, weren't you?"

"Yes."

"Well, you probably wouldn't understand what it's like to be raised by an alcoholic father and a nagging Christian mother in a rat-infested flat in the South Side of Chicago. You wouldn't know what it is like to watch your four brothers end up in prison and your five sisters involved in prostitution.

"One day I told my father, when he staggered into the house and beat my mother, that I wished he were dead. My mother always tried to get me to go to church with her, but I could see that religion wasn't helping her poverty and poor marriage. I told her that Christianity was an 'opium for the poor.' Her heart was broken by that comment, but she continued, as before, to pray for me to one day 'find Jesus as my personal Savior.' I can still hear her saying those words.

"I vowed to myself that I was going to rise above that poverty, become a doctor, and help those people in my neighborhood. As a matter of fact, the neighborhood was so excited to hear my plans, they established a special education fund for my college and medical school expenses. They did request that I sign a pledge to practice medicine there for at least five years after graduation from medical school.

"During college and medical school days, I became so comfortable with middle-class living, that I didn't want to go back to that poverty-stricken neighborhood. I stayed in Peoria and tried to ignore the frequent letters from my former neighborhood leaders. I established a well-paying practice here in Peoria and tried to forget about the poverty of my youth. Everything was going all right until about two years ago. I have this burden, this load, which is so heavy. I can't carry it anymore. My family and medical practice are in a shambles. I don't have the strength, and I'm not sure I even have the desire, to try to put things back together."

Bob said, "I believe you do want to put things back together. But you must go back and establish new foundations in your own life." Bob proceeded to counsel David about guilt. The guilt David felt was because of his sin against his family, his parents, and his neighborhood. Bob went on to inform David that all sin committed against people is also committed against God. Bob was able to show David the way of release from guilt. David would have to confess his sin and ask forgiveness from his parents, his neighborhood leaders, his wife, his children, and God. David was hesitant about asking others for forgiveness. He had never done that in all his life! But he felt that drawing, magnetic power again to do what was right, which he later realized was the working of the Holy Spirit.

David began laying new foundations by repenting of his sin against God, asking for His forgiveness, and inviting Jesus Christ to come into his heart to be Lord and Master. He asked forgiveness from his wife, children, parents, and neighborhood leaders. David moved his family and medical practice back to the old neighborhood. His income is far less, but the relief of being forgiven more than makes up for the loss. His greatest joy was when he led his father to receive that same forgiveness from God which he had experienced. David had certainly experienced the destructive forces of guilt. But he also knows the joy of forgiveness.

What Is Guilt?

What is this destructive force which every human being experiences? "In psychology, guilt can be defined as a realization that one has violated ethical, moral, or religious principles, together with a resulting feeling of regret and lessened personal worth."[1] Guilt is the result of self-blame. Every rational person feels guilt at one time or another; some to a lesser or greater degree than others. One person might not feel much guilt. When he receives too much change from the store clerk, he can walk away with a feeling of jubilance. Another person loses sleep, appetite, and even personal happiness, if he does not return the excess change given by the cashier.

Historians say that Abraham Lincoln, as a youth, walked many miles to return a few pennies to a man who had given him too much change. His strict ethical, moral, and religious principles led Lincoln to be called "Honest Abe." What caused Lincoln to be honest in his dealings and to be so sensitive to his guilt? He, like every other rational human being, had a storehouse of principles—a conscience—put into his mind through the efforts of his parents, teachers, friends, preachers, and life experiences. These principles, composed of ethical, moral, and religious information, govern the decision making of the individual. When a person makes a choice against those principles, the conscience is wounded and guilt results.

There is a real problem when it comes to acting in accordance to these principles stored in the mind. Because of man's fallen and rebellious nature toward God, the information that springs from the conscience is not always reliable. The apostle Paul spoke of this unreliability of the conscience when answering to the dictates of the old, fallen nature of man: "For the good that I would I do not: but the evil which I would not, that I do" (Rom. 7:19).

God gives to every person who has a personal faith in Jesus Christ a new, reliable nature. This new nature is our union with the resurrected Christ, activated by the Holy Spirit indwelling all born-again believers. Jesus said, ". . . If any man thirst, let him come unto me, and drink. He that believeth on me, as the scripture hath said, out of his belly shall flow rivers of living water. (But this spake he of the Spirit, which they that believe on him should receive . . .)" (John 7:37–39). The Holy Spirit enables the Christian's conscience to be reliable in weighing out ethical, moral, and religious principles, and in making the right decisions. The moving of the Holy Spirit upon the conscience makes the Christian walk many miles to take some pennies back to their rightful owner. When the Christian grieves the Holy Spirit by sin, faulty decisions are made and guilt abounds.

Some psychologists attempt to categorize guilt into types. "False guilt," they say, arises when we are only aware that our behavior or thoughts go against what society expects of us. We feel guilty only because we have acted inappropriately in a social setting. One author put it: "When we feel guilty because we have wasted time, made a sarcastic remark, or acted in some other socially undesirable way, we experience false guilt. True guilt, in contrast, is the result of disobedience to God and a failure to act in accordance with His standards."[2]

David, King of Israel, experienced true guilt. He indulged in his own self-will and lust, which caused him to commit adultery and murder, and he was overburdened with guilt. He certainly had violated what society deemed proper! Yet in his prayer of repentance, in Psalm 51:4, David said to God, "Against thee, thee only, have I sinned, and done this evil in thy sight. . . ." David knew that all sin, whether against a neighbor or directly against God, is a violation of God's standards. Any violation of God's standards, whether learned from the Bible or from the principles of society, will cause the wounded conscience to produce guilt.

Not all people feel an equal amount of guilt for wrongdoing. Some bank robbers feel very little guilt about frightening bank employees and stealing money which belongs to other people. Yet, many people are so sensitive to their conscience that if they let the slightest infraction of a moral, ethical, or religious code go unconfessed, they will experience heavy guilt. What makes the difference between those who are sensitive to guilt and others who are not? Making the conscience callous by suppressing guilt will desensitize it. The guilt is still there, it just is not *felt* anymore. Callousing the conscience does not rid a person of guilt. The guilt eventually surfaces as emotional or physical illness. *It never goes away.*

A man in Minneapolis sent the following note to the Great Northern Railway:

Gentlemen:
Many years ago when a youngster of high school age,
I stole a ride of about two hundred miles on a box car
of one of your trains. A few years later I rode your
coach train one station further than my ticket called
for. This has troubled my conscience all these years
(47 of them). Here is payment for the rides with six
percent compound interest, and asking to be forgiven
for the long delay. [sic][3]

That man realized, after forty-seven years of suppressing his guilt, that it would never leave unless
dealt with in the right way. He gave restitution and
asked for forgiveness in order to be released from the
forty-seven-year torture of guilt.

Guilt can arise from two separate areas of one's life.
Gary Collins identifies these areas as the *guilt of doing*
and the *guilt of being*.[4]

"The guilt of doing is a feeling of remorse which
arises because we have done something to hurt
another person or to alienate us from others. This
was seen in Shakespeare's *Macbeth*, where both of the
murderers suffered intense guilt reactions after the
death of King Duncan. Macbeth responded with hal-
lucinations while Lady Macbeth began sleepwalking
and a compulsive wringing of her hands."[5]

Guilt of doing can be produced by committing any
transgression against the moral, ethical, or religious
codes of others. Burnout victims are frequently in
violation of these principles at work and at home. The
guilt surfaces in the burnout victim's conscience and
then is often quickly suppressed. This suppressed
guilt adds to the misery of all the other feelings of
despair, discouragement, and hopelessness.

The guilt of being "is a feeling of remorse which comes from the realization that one is disobedient and at odds with the will of God."[6] The guilt of being does not say to you, "There is something wrong with your job." Instead, it says, "There is something wrong with you!" The guilt of being is designed to cause a person to look inward in self-examination and upward to heaven for confession. What causes the conscience to produce this kind of guilt? It comes from exposure to the Scriptures (see 2 Tim. 3:16), exposure to preaching (see Acts 2:37), and through the work of the Holy Spirit on the conscience itself (see Rom. 1:18,19).

King David of Israel committed sins which produced both the guilt of doing and the guilt of being. He tried to hide his guilt of adultery with Bathsheba and the murder of her husband Uriah. One day the prophet Nathan told David a parable which caused David to judge himself. God's messenger had made David's conscience sensitive to guilt. The fifty-first Psalm is the account of David's guilt feelings and what he did about them. In verse 3, David speaks about the weight of his sin and guilt: ". . . My sin is ever before me," he said.

Burnout victims usually ask themselves, "Why me? Why do I feel so bad about my job and myself?" Jay Adams, author, teacher, and counselor, says, "Most people know why they are in trouble, even when at first they deny it."[7] Guilt keeps the transgression ever clear in the mind. People filled with self-pity who ask, "Why me?" are usually wanting pity from others instead of help.

God has built within man's conscience an awareness of sin. It is like the seat belt buzzer in a car that "sounds off" when the driver fails to buckle up. The seat belt buzzer shuts off after a few seconds if ignored. The conscience, unlike the seat belt buzzer, continues to emit warnings to the mind whether ignored or not. This soon becomes mental torture. The guilt of the burnout victim permeates every thought. It does not go away. God intended for man's conscience to force the person into confronting the guilt. Dealing with it is the only release.

Face to Face With Guilt

So how do you deal with guilt when you have burned out? I found that in my own Christian life, I had to make two lists: First, a list of offenses that others had committed against me, and second, a list of offenses that I had committed.

This is an important procedure any time you are dealing with guilt. List the offenses of your employer, your supervisor, or any other person who you feel has contributed to your burnout. Those offenses could be unrealistic expectations and demands, favoritism, lack of understanding, isolation, or broken promises. List every offense that comes to mind.

Now, list all of *your* offenses which have been committed at work and at home before, during, and after your burnout. This takes some soul-searching, because most people tend to hide their own sins while emphasizing the wrongs of others. Begin by asking God to turn on His spotlight in your mind. Ask Him to uncover every offense, even the smallest ones. When God begins to expose those sins, you will be astounded at the number and variety. Most often, they will include poor attitude, ungratefulness, stubbornness, lying, cheating, bitterness, or envy. Write them all down, even though the task is difficult. In mulling over your past you will remember specific instances of wrongdoing, and those should be put on your list as well.

Now, review both lists. Identify the *basic* offense committed against you by your employer and those around you, and then your *basic* offense. Your employer's *basic* offense could be insensitivity. Your *basic* offense could be a poor attitude. If all the other offenses seem to branch out from one offense, then that one is the *basic* offense.

The next step is confession and, if necessary, restitution. Confession means to say the same thing about your sin that God says about it. Confess your sin—your basic offense and all that goes with it—to God and ask His forgiveness. Then, go to your employer or supervisor and ask for forgiveness. This task is not easy to do, but God will give you the power to do that which seems impossible! Ask for forgiveness, and in a loving spirit forgive the offenses committed against you. Don't draw attention to the things for which you are forgiving your employer or supervisor. That is not the attitude of true forgiveness. Such an attitude will only cause conflict and another situation from which more guilt might arise. Forgiving means to forget. God has said He removes our transgressions as far as the east is from the west (see Ps. 103:12).

If your employer is not a Christian, don't be surprised if the reaction is negative. You are not responsible for his or her response. Your call is to obedience. True forgiveness means that the past point of conflict does not bother you anymore, not even when you meet the person who caused the conflict.

Is getting rid of guilt worth all that humiliation? Yes! Release from guilt is the only answer to a healthy mental and physical state for a victim of burnout. The person who refuses to face this guilt problem and resolve the conflicts which started it, will, more than likely, never resolve future conflicts. He will always be on the run, always trying to leave problems in the past with the hope that there will be no problems in the future. No one can ever run away from his conscience.

Notes

1. H. B. English and A. C. English, *A Comprehensive Dictionary of Psychological and Psychoanalytical Terms* (New York: Longmans, Green, 1958), p. 234.
2. Gary R. Collins, *Man in Motion* (Carol Stream, Ill.: Creation House, 1973), p. 137.

3. Gary R. Collins, *Fractured Personalities* (Carol Stream, Ill.: Creation House, 1972), p. 28.
4. Ibid., p. 27.
5. Ibid.
6. Ibid., p. 29.
7. Jay E. Adams, *Competent to Counsel* (Phillipsburg, N.J.: Presbyterian and Reformed Publishing Company, 1974), p. 117.

6

A Living Time Bomb

The radio alarm clicked on, and the announcer, with his trumpet voice, blared, "Get up! Get up! What do you think this is, your birthday?"

Chad rolled over, struck the radio with a karate chop, and vowed, "Tonight I will definitely find a different station to wake me up."

It had not been a restful night for Chad Wilson. He had been exhausted when he went to bed, but he hardly slept all night. He stumbled to the bathroom, looked into the mirror, and said, "Just look at me! I've only had this job for one year, and I look ten years older than when I started working for the paper."

Chad was sensitive about his appearance. As a high school student in Iowa, he won the hearts of most of the girls in his class. At Northwestern University, where he majored in journalism, he was the heart throb of many sorority women. While working for a sports magazine for two years in Chicago, Chad was frequently a guest on TV talk shows. His achievement as "Sportswriter of the Year" and his good looks opened many doors of opportunity for him. A TV interview had landed him the offer of his current job, a sportswriter with a Los Angeles newspaper.

"The good ole days are gone," said Chad, as he gazed in the mirror at those stress lines on his face. Those lines were but a fraction of Chad's worries. He was constantly fatigued. No amount of rest seemed to help. He retired early in the evening when he did not have to work late, yet he always woke up absolutely worn out. Some nights he could not sleep at all. His fingers had stopped typing his latest interview, but his mind typed that story all night long.

But that was not all that was wrong with the twenty-eight-year-old reporter. Chad began experiencing frequent vomiting and diarrhea, especially after his editor gave him one of those "deadline or else" ultimatums. Chad knew these symptoms were not the flu. He had had them for a month, and they were getting worse.

"Well, as much as I hate to, I'd better get ready for work," said Chad. His every motion was one of drudgery. As he walked down the stairs from his apartment, he wondered if he would have the strength to walk to his car. He walked by the parking lot attendant, who was sitting in his little booth with his feet propped up. Chad thought, *Now, there is a man who really has it made. He has no deadlines to meet, no editor screaming at him, no competition from anybody, no stress at all. What a job!*

By the time he reached the freeway, Chad had already put his mind behind his typewriter at work. *I know the new stadium story is going to break today,* he thought. *I've spent two weeks digging up the information*

on this story. Maybe I can get the editor to accept it today.
He'd better not tell me to get more facts!

Chad walked into the sports department, a large, noisy room which he shared with nineteen other reporters. He picked up the morning paper on his desk. There it was in the headlines—his story was on the front page. But he hadn't written it yet! He looked at the byline. "Jim Wells! Who gave him the right to report my story?" yelled Chad as he stormed from his desk to the editor's office. He pushed open the door and shook the newspaper in front of the editor's face. "Just tell me why you did this to me? All I want is a good explanation!" screamed Chad.

The stone-faced, stern-voiced editor said, "You're slipping, Chad. Something is wrong with you. I had Wells work on the story too, just in case you came apart at the seams. The story just happened to break last night. It happened right after you got sick and went home. Sorry, Chad, you know this business is competitive."

Stunned by the editor's comments, Chad stumbled from desk to desk as he made his way to the restroom. He became so sick that the continual vomiting caused him to become dizzy. He fell to the floor, hitting his head on the sink, and lost consciousness. When Chad woke up, he was in a hospital emergency room. He faced several weeks of psychotherapy, strong medicines, and a special diet.

That tragedy was the turning point in Chad's life and career. A psychologist at the hospital had several sessions of informative discussion with Chad about stress and its effects. When Chad was discharged from the hospital, he quit his job with the Los

Angeles paper, moved back to Chicago, and managed to get his old job back with the sports magazine. Chad would always bear the scars of burnout.

There are many Chads in the working world, paying dearly for their high achievements. These hundreds of thousands and maybe even millions of Chads are saying to themselves, "Just look at me," as they see the physical consequences of over-stress and burnout.

The Type A Person

Physicians are discovering that certain behavior patterns and lifestyles bring on mental and physical health problems. Doctors Meyer Friedman and Ray H. Rosenman, in their book, *Type A Behavior and Your Heart*, describe the "Type A person as one who is geared up for health problems. Type A Behavior Pattern is an action-emotion complex that can be observed in any person who is aggressively involved in a chronic, incessant struggle to achieve more and more in less and less time, and if required to do so, against the opposing efforts of other things or other persons."[1]

The Type A person is like a bomb needing only a fuse and a match. The stress-filled, high-achievement environment is the fuse. The fuse is lit when the Type A person begins to experience certain problems, which are revealed by the symptoms of Type A behavior. Friedman and Rosenman list thirteen of them.

1. Explosively accentuating various key words in your ordinary speech . . . , and a tendency to

utter the last few words of your sentences far more rapidly than the opening words.

2. You always move, walk, and eat rapidly.

3. You feel an impatience with the rate at which most events take place.

4. You indulge in polyphasic thought or performance, frequently striving to think of or do two or more things simultaneously.

5. You always find it difficult to refrain from talking about or bringing the theme of any conversation around to those subjects which especially interest and intrigue you . . . .

6. You almost *always* feel vaguely guilty when you relax and do absolutely nothing for several hours to several days.

7. You no longer observe the more important or interesting or lovely objects that you encounter in your milieu.

8. You do not have any time to spare to become the things worth *being* because you are so preoccupied with getting the things worth *having*.

9. You attempt to schedule more and more in less and less time.

10. On meeting another severely afflicted Type A person, instead of feeling compassion for his affliction you find yourself compelled to "challenge" him.

11. You resort to certain characteristic gestures or nervous tics.

12. You believe that whatever success you have enjoyed has been due in good part to your ability to get things done faster than your fellowmen.

13. You find yourself increasingly and ineluctably committed to translating and evaluating not only your own but also the activities of others in terms of "numbers."[2]

My own life was a clear example of these symptoms. I always walked faster than the rest of the family. I constantly rushed twenty paces ahead of them without realizing it. I shoveled my food down as quickly as possible, always finishing before the others did. I always said, "It's a habit from seminary days when I only had ten minutes to eat my meals."

I indulged in polyphasic thought quite frequently. Sometimes I thought of a meeting I was about to attend, while somebody was already talking with me. I even used to do this from the pulpit! One weekend I was setting up a darkroom in our home and struggling with a problem in the layout. Sunday morning, right in the middle of my sermon, the solution to the darkroom popped into my mind. There I was, preaching salvation and thinking photography!

I was a Type A person through and through. But, through God's grace, an understanding church, and much prayer, I have made the transition (for the most part) to a Type B person.

Type B Person

Friedman and Rosenman suggest that they have discovered another pattern of behavior, the Type B pattern.

The person with Type B Behavior Pattern is the exact opposite of the Type A subject. He, unlike the Type A person, is rarely harried by desire to obtain a wildly increasing number of things or participate in an endlessly growing series of events in an ever decreasing amount of time. His intelligence may be as good as or even better than that of the Type A subject. Similarly, his ambition may be as great or even greater than that of his Type A counterpart. He may also have a considerable amount of "drive," but its character is such that it seems to steady him, give confidence and security to him, rather than to goad, irritate, and infuriate, as with the Type A man.[3]

How does one know if he or she is a Type B person? Friedman and Rosenman have a brief list of identifying factors for the Type B person too.

1. You are completely free of all the habits and exhibit none of the traits we have listed that harass the severely afflicted Type A person.
2. You never suffer from a sense of time urgency with its accompanying impatience.
3. You harbor no free-floating hostility, and you feel no need to display or discuss either your achievements or accomplishments unless such exposure is demanded by the situation.
4. When you play, you do so to find fun and relaxation, not to exhibit your superiority at any cost.
5. You can relax without guilt, just as you can work without agitation.[4]

The Hurry Sickness

The conclusion of Friedman and Rosenman is that the "hurry sickness" which plagues the Type A person leads to definite physical problems, especially heart attack. Other physicians agree. Dr. C. D.

Jenkins, in the *New England Journal of Medicine,* said: "The psychosocial viewpoint considers premature death from coronary heart disease to be the result of a complex of interacting factors, including environmental, psychological, social, constitutional, and behavioral characteristics of the individual."[5]

How does Type A behavior and job dissatisfaction bring about health problems?

> Prolonged dissatisfaction may produce permanent activation of biochemical mechanisms, such as persistent essential hypertension and increased heart rate, or it may be associated with abnormal elevation of blood chemistry, such as serum cholesterol or triglycerides. Permanent activation of these arousal mechanisms may cause stress to the circulatory system and, as a result, cause premature death from coronary disease.[6]

Approaching a job with Type A behavior and remaining on the same job after burnout has taken place causes the body's systems to be hyperactive all the time. This is one reason that people in either situation have difficulty sleeping. The body might be inactive—even worn out—but the mind continues at the same rapid pace.

This hurry sickness was a serious problem for me when I burned out. Many times I brought work home from the office and pored over it until late at night. When I went to bed, my mind was still working. I sermonized, made up bulletins, and handled correspondence in my sleep! My body was exhausted, but my mind was running full throttle.

One night I was awakened by a severe pain in my colon. I had never had such a pain before. I felt as if my insides were caught in a muscle spasm. I got out of bed, walked around, and the pain soon went away. A few days later I experienced the same sensation, and then it happened again. I endured several painful and expensive tests only to learn that a spastic colon was the price I was paying for being a Type A person. Every time I was under stress, or if something went wrong at a board meeting, these spasms would recur. They always hit about one hour after I retired for the evening. My mind was harassing my body, trying to get the message across that it was not allowed to rest. I endured this thorn in the flesh for almost six years. Only when I dealt with my negative stress and Type A behavior did the muscle spasms dissipate.

The Mental Price

Herbert Freudenberger, a psychoanalyst mentioned earlier, has compiled a list of mental problems associated with burnout.

1. *Exhaustion:* Loss of energy and the accompanying feelings of weariness . . .
2. *Detachment:* . . . you separate yourself from the people and events; you strip them of their power to hurt you.
3. *Boredom and Cynicism:* You begin to question the value of activities and friendships, even of life itself. You become skeptical of people's motives and blasé about causes.

4. *Impatience and Heightened Irritability:* Flare-ups occur that seem totally out of character as the Burn-Out blames his family and co-workers for things that were more his fault than theirs.

5. *A Sense of Omnipotence:* "Nobody else can do it; only I can."

6. *Suspicion of Being Unappreciated:* He feels aggrieved at the lack of appreciation people are showing toward him. After all, they're leaving early; he's staying late. He gets bitter and increasingly angry.

7. *Paranoia:* When things are going wrong, a vague feeling sets in that someone must be at fault. The boss, co-workers, a spouse, a child—anyone handy will serve as a target.

8. *Disorientation:* His cognitive powers will suffer—not from "old age" or "senility," as he may jokingly remark, but from the agitation he's creating inside himself. His speech patterns will falter as he finds himself forgetting what he started to say. Names and dates will elude him. His concentration span will be much more limited.

9. *Psychosomatic Complaints:* Headaches, colds that linger, backaches—all may be signs that something is wrong.

10. *Depression:* There are differences between a generally depressed state and the form of depression that signifies Burn-Out. In a non-related depression, the condition is prolonged and pervades all areas of a person's life. In a Burn-Out, the depression is usually temporary, specific and localized, pertaining more or less to one area of life. While a generally depressed person is likely to feel profound guilt for everything going wrong, the Burn-Out is more apt to be angry.[7]

102

Maybe you recognize some of your feelings in this list. If your job is bringing about these changes in your mental attitude, then admit this is happening to you. "The real danger in Burn-Out is non-feeling, the denial that anything is wrong. As soon as denial enters the picture, the person's symptoms become enemies instead of allies. No matter how loudly they cry out, no one is listening."[8]

There are hundreds of thousands of burned out, Type A people who are not listening to their physical and mental warning signals. Many burned out people believe that things will get better with time. Others simply consider their physical and mental symptoms as weaknesses which need to be overcome.

One who is burned out must be able to sense and understand what has happened to his or her health, mental attitude, job, and especially what destruction has been done to family, friends, and co-workers. Facing the truth is a giant step toward recovery from burnout. *Burnout is reversible, no matter how advanced it is,* but the physical and mental effects might not be.

Set your mind right now to recognize your condition. Seek help for the *cause* of your burnout, not just the *effects* (this will be discussed at length in Chapters 8 and 9). Then determine to make some changes in your attitude. Most of all, seek to change that main point of agitation which caused the burnout. Don't try to run away from your problems. A world without problems is a world without progress or people. Face reality and deal with that thorn in your flesh.

Don't refuse to face up to the physical and mental

anguish of burnout. It will not go away on its own. Avoidance of dealing with burnout will only continue the mental and physical harm to yourself and others. The next chapter is the voice of loved ones speaking about the hurt caused by people who will not deal with their burnout problems.

Notes

1. Meyer Friedman, M.D. and Ray H. Rosenman, M.D., *Type A Behavior and Your Heart* (Greenwich, Conn.: Faw-cett Publications, 1974), p. 84.
2. Ibid., pp. 100–102.
3. Ibid., pp. 84,85.
4. Ibid., p. 103.
5. C. D. Jenkins, "Psychological and Social Precursors of Coronary Disease," *New England Journal of Medicine* 284 (1971), p. 244.
6. "Job Dissatisfaction," *Intellect*, May–June, 1976, p. 596.
7. Herbert J. Freudenberger, "Don't burn out: Prevent or Cure it," *Indianapolis Star*, Nov. 23, 1980, Sec. 7, p. 4. (For an in-depth study of the mental effects of burnout see Dr. Freudenberger's book, *Burnout: The High Cost of*

Achievement (Garden City, N.Y.: Anchor-Doubleday, 1980), pp. 61–67.

8. Ibid.

7

Unrighteous Indignation

The effects of burnout are not isolated to its victims. No one knows this better than the families of burned out workers who have been ruined by this dreaded stress disease. Fellow workers suffer obliquely from the burned out employee, supervisor, or executive. They suffer from his or her impatience, nonappreciativeness, impersonal attitudes, and verbal abuses. But the fellow worker feels little of the devastating effects of being near someone who is burned out. The family catches the full force of his or her unrighteous indignation.

Sociologists Murray Straus, Richard Gelles, and Suzanne Steinmetz estimate that

30 percent of all married couples have had at least one violent episode during their marriage.

In one year, some 1.8 million wives are severely attacked by their husbands—and almost the same number of husbands are assaulted by their wives. Women, however, sustain the more serious injuries.

Nearly 2 million children a year (almost 4 percent of all children from three to seventeen) are victims of parental abuse and neglect. (H.H.S. reports that 2,000 die as a result).

In addition, the F.B.I. reports that in 1978 one out of every five murder victims was killed by a family member.[1]

One should not assume that all of these statistics of family abuse represent cases of burned out people abusing their families. Most victims of burnout are never violent at all. They are either sullen or use mental or verbal abuse against their loved ones. Many family abusers learned their abusive tendencies from their parents and did not become abusive because of burnout.

Studies have documented that families pass on a heritage of violence to succeeding generations. Child abusers tend to have been abused as children, and parents who are violent to each other are more likely than nonviolent parents to have children who use violence on siblings, schoolmates, and later on, their own spouses.[2]

However, many sociologists believe that the burned out worker is responsible for much family abuse. Family abuse can be mental, verbal, or physical. Women who burn out are less likely to abuse their families physically.

Frequently, a woman experiencing severe job stress looks for an excessive amount of support from her husband or partner, thus putting pressure on the marriage or relationship, which often fails shortly after . . . . Such a woman becomes less willing to iron out domestic discord or to listen to family members' problems. Her husband and children may feel neglected and hurt by her lack of attention and subsequently withdraw from her.[3]

Although burned out women usually use mental or verbal abuse on their families, instead of physical abuse, the result is still severe: The family disintegrates.

Burned out men are not always violent with their families. Instead, they may withdraw completely emotionally. Whenever I had an exhausting day and felt emotionally drained, I wanted to be alone. I took long walks or secluded myself away from others for several hours. I suppose I thought that since interaction with people had caused my anguish, I just wouldn't interact with anyone. I am certain that my times alone were abusive to my family. They had needs which could only be met by a husband or a father. Where was I when they needed me? Taking long walks!

The burned out ministers I interviewed were not violent with their families, except one. But their moods were often fierce. One pastor told me that when he comes home after a difficult board meeting even the dog knows where to hide!

When burned out men use physical violence on their families, it is often extreme. It is not unusual for a wife to be the object of her husband's stress-related wrath. The husband comes home late from work, is uptight, and needs an emotional release from his stress. His wife is usually handy.

I have found in my counseling of problem marriages that men allow their frustrations to build up to such an extent that they simply blow up and take those frustrations out on their wives, who happen to be the closest targets. In this way men maintain an illusion of control in their own households, to counteract their knowledge that the rest of their lives are coming apart.

Many wives and children live in constant, often paralyzing, terror of that husband and father who is suffering from burnout. One eleven-year-old said, "I stay out of Dad's way when he gets home. If he just sees me, I'll get it."[4]

Just the Ordinary Guy

People who are burned out and abusive come from all walks of life. If a man experiences burnout, he has the potential to take out his frustrations on his wife and children. The following are but two of the incidents I encountered as a counselor (sometimes referee) to troubled people.

Judy was thirty, married to a highway patrolman, and the mother of two small children. She was a new Christian, but her husband Doug was a devout atheist. Shortly after she accepted Christ as her personal Savior, Doug began to grow cold to her. He told her that she wasn't any "fun" to be around anymore, now that she was a Christian.

Doug's jobs were difficult and demanding. Not only did he work eight hours per day as a patrolman; he also moonlighted for another eight hours each night as a security guard for a local factory. He was burned out and filled with hatred. That hatred exploded late one night like the burst of a cannon. Judy was the target.

I saw Judy the next day. Her cheek was bruised and one of her eyes was black and swollen. Her first reaction was to think of divorce. But after biblical counseling she realized that divorce was not the answer.

Judy was able to help Doug once she understood that he was burned out. She encouraged him to seek different employment. Doug did find a different and less stressful line of police work. Judy also found a part-time job for herself in order to lighten her husband's work load. Judy is no longer being abused.

Another incident of abuse involved a son and his mother. A fifty-year-old woman burst into my office one day and told me that her twenty-eight-year-old son had beaten her. When he left to get a gun to kill her, she fled from her home and ran to my office.

Mother and son had lived together ever since he had divorced his wife. He was a burned out, unemployed salesman. The unemployment and his mother's nagging about his laziness finally became too much for him.

I had to have the authorities incarcerate the son until the mother could pack her belongings. We then helped her move over one thousand miles away. Here was an instance in which a man paid a very high price due to burnout. He will probably never see his mother again.

It is believed that violence in the family is a direct result of stress. "Most violent families are those under the greatest stress."[5]

At the root of many of these incidents, say authorities, are money and job worries and the inability to cope with an increasingly complicated world. Recent studies also trace part of the violence to the resentment some men feel toward new advances made by women both at work and in society at large.[6]

Unrighteous indignation, or sinful anger, allows the enemies of the soul to attack and greatly influence that person's rationale. The Bible says, "He that hath no rule over his own spirit is like a city that is broken down, and without walls" (Prov. 25:28). An ancient city which had neither soldiers nor fortification stood little chance of keeping out the enemy. The angry, burned out husband or wife knocks down all defenses for the maintaining of rational conduct. When the walls of love and concern are flattened by discouragement, depression, and self-pity, then the person behind those walls will be conquered by the enemy. The enemy is the God-hating, rebellious, and fallen nature of man influenced by Satan. If allowed to have control, the fallen nature of man has this potential: ". . . adultery, fornication, uncleanness, lasciviousness, idolatry, witchcraft, hatred, variance, emulations, wrath, strife, seditions, heresies, envyings, murders, drunkenness, revellings . . ." (Gal. 5:19–21).

My firm belief is that *burnout breaks down the walls of defense.* Burnout allows the enemy to march into one's life and take control. The persons and things once loved are now hated or abused. Many burned out men love their families, yet still abuse them. A man might even say to his wife and children after a beating, "You might not think I love you, but I do." He might also say, "Something comes over me when I feel strife at home. It is like something inside me takes control, and I just seem helpless to stop my anger.'

Burnout and family abuse compose a vicious and violent cycle. The stress at work produces stress in the home, which puts more stress back on the job. Finally the anger from the job is transferred to the home. There it explodes in violence, harm, and tragedy. It is not unusual to hear of the "model" employee, filled with stress-related anger, who goes home, shoots his family, goes back to work, kills his employer, then turns the gun on himself. A few victims of burnout believe violence is the only way to solve a problem of that magnitude. That is not the way!

Help for the Abuser and the Abused

If you are abusing your family mentally, physically or emotionally—or if you are being abused—seek help! Thousands of people in this country are trained to give assistance to the abuser and the abused. Don't be afraid to admit that this tragedy is happening. A counselor can help you break the vicious cycle which is destroying you and your family.

First and foremost, seek help through your church. If your pastor is unable to help you personally, ask him to recommend counsel elsewhere. If you are not active currently in a Christian congregation, look for a church that is firmly committed to Jesus Christ as

Lord—one that takes the Holy Scriptures and the historic Christian faith seriously.

Second, make the daily reading of the Scriptures and personal prayer a vital part of your schedule. The Psalms will be especially helpful and encouraging. Ask God to work the necessary changes in your life which are needed to solve the problems facing you. No doubt you have trusted Him before in other areas which appeared to be impossible. Unlike us, Jesus Christ cannot fail. Look to Him in this area of need. "Surely he hath borne our griefs, and carried our sorrows . . ." (Is. 53:4). Only He can ultimately heal our burnout and despair.

If you are faced with an immediate emergency and need on-the-spot help from a social agency, a list of possible organizations to contact is given at the end of this chapter.[7]

It is important to realize that most of these organizations probably will not approach the problem with a Christian understanding. Many family therapists attempt to help abusers and the abused to solve their problems without any spiritual assistance. I repeat: Competent Christian counsel should be sought, either before or in conjunction with the agencies commissioned by the government. Contact the pastor of a Bible-believing church for direction to competent Christian counsel.

Innocent family members should not have to suffer because of a worker's unresolved stress. All persons concerned must seek immediate help. Stress-related family abuse demands a total commitment to resolve it. Action must be taken. It will not go away by itself.

NATIONAL ORGANIZATIONS

Center for Women Policy Studies
(CWPS)
2000 P Street, N.W., Suite 508
Washington, D.C. 20036

Domestic Violence and Spouse
Assault Project, Inc.
1917 Washtenaw Avenue
Ann Arbor, Mich. 48104

Family Violence Research
Program
Sociology Department
University of New Hampshire
Durham, N.H. 03824

Women in Crisis
444 Park Avenue South
New York, N.Y. 10016

Women's Rights Program Unit
U.S. Commission on Civil
Rights
1121 Vermont Avenue, N.W.
Washington, D.C. 20425

LOCAL ORGANIZATIONS

Rainbow Retreat, Inc.
4332 North 12th Street
Phoenix, Ariz. 85014
(Mainly for alcohol-related
abuse.)

Mothers In Stress Service
(M.I.S.S.)
1147 Ohio Street
Fairfield, Calif. 94533

Solano Center for Battered
Women
P.O. Box 2051
Fairfield, Calif. 94533

Women Shelter
P.O. Box 4222
Long Beach, Calif. 90804

Women's Transitional Living
Center, Inc.
P.O. Box 6103
Orange, Calif. 92667

Haven House, Inc.
P.O. Box 2007
Pasadena, Calif. 91105
(Mainly for alcohol-related
abuse.)

La Casa De Las Madres
P.O. Box 15147
San Francisco, Calif. 94115

York Street Center
1632 York Street
Denver, Colo. 80260

Women in Crisis Center Shelter
1426 Pierce Street
Lakewood, Colo. 80214

Prudence Crandall Center for Women
Box 895
New Britain, Conn. 06050

House of Ruth Annex
1215 New Jersey Street, N.W.
Washington, D.C. 20001

Hubbard House
1231 Hubbard Street
Jacksonville, Fla. 32206

Dade County Task Force on Battered Women
100 Southeast Fourth Street
Miami, Fla. 33131

Shelter for Abused Spouses and Children
1888 Owawa Street
Honolulu, Hawaii 96819

The Salvation Army
The Emergency Lodge
432 W. Wisconsin Street
Chicago, Ill. 60614

Rosie's Place
23 Dartmouth Street
Boston, Mass. 02116

Transition House
c/o Woman's Center
46 Pleasant Street
Cambridge, Mass. 02139

Elizabeth Stone House
128 Minden Street
Jamaica Plain, Mass. 02130

Respond
P.O. Box 555
Somerville, Mass. 02143

Abby's House
23 Crown Street
Worcester, Mass. 01608

Domestic Violence and Spouse Assault Project, Inc.
1917 Washtenaw Avenue
Ann Arbor, Mich. 48104

Rape/Spouse Assault Crisis Center
29 Strong Avenue
Muskegon, Mich. 49441

Women's Advocates
584 Grand Avenue
St. Paul, Minn. 55102

Center for the Elimination of Violence in the Family, Inc.
P.O. Box 279
Bay Ridge Station
Brooklyn, N.Y. 11220

Victims Information Bureau of Suffolk (VIBS)
501 Route 111
Hauppauge, N.Y. 11787

Hofstra Center for Physically or Psychologically Abused Women
Hofstra University
Hempstead, N.Y. 11550

Abused Women's Aid in Crisis
G.P.O. Box 1699
New York, N.Y. 10001

Partners Anonymous
158-18 Riverside Drive
New York, N.Y. 10032

Vera House, Inc.
P.O. Box 62
Syracuse, N.Y. 13207

Akron Task Force on Battered Women, Inc.
146 South High Street
Akron, Ohio 44308

Project Woman
22 East Grand Avenue
Springfield, Ohio 45506

Bradley-Angle House
P.O. Box 40132
Portland, Ore. 97240

National Organization for Women (NOW)
Task Force on Household Violence/Battered Women
P.O. Box 843
Portland, Ore. 97207

Women in Crisis, Inc.
Harrisburg, Pa. 17101
(Full address withheld upon request)

Women Against Abuse
Emergency Shelter
P.O. Box 12233
Philadelphia, Pa. 19144

Women's Center South
6907 Frankstown Avenue
Pittsburgh, Pa. 15208

YWCA Crisis Center
300 8th Street
Chattanooga, Tenn. 37403

*Women's Shelter & Support
Service Program*
Y.W.C.A.
220 East Union
Olympia, Wash. 98501

Catherine Booth House
The Salvation Army
925 East Pike Street
Seattle, Wash. 98122

*Young Women's Christian
Association Battered Women's
Program*
West 829 Broadway Avenue
Spokane, Wash. 99201

*Y.W.C.A. Women's Emergency
House*
1012 West 12th Street
Vancouver, Wash. 98660

Task Force on Battered Women
3719 West Fond du Lac
Avenue
Milwaukee, Wis. 53216

*Calgary Women's Emergency
Shelter Association*
938 15th Avenue, S.W.
Calgary, Alberta
Canada

Ishtar Transition House
Langley, British Columbia
Canada
(Address withheld upon
request)

*Auberge Transition/Transition
House*
1355 Dorchester Street West
Montreal, Quebec H3G 1T3
Canada

Interval House
211-5th Avenue North
Saskatoon, Saskatchewan
Canada

*Women in Transition
Incorporated*
143 Spadina Road
Toronto, Ontario M5R 2T1
Canada

Transition House
c/o Vancouver Status of
Women
2029 West Fourth Avenue
Vancouver, British Columbia
V6J 1N3
Canada

117

Chiswick Women's Aid
369 Chiswick High Road
London W4, England

National Women's Aid
Federation
51, Chalcot Road
London NW 1, England

Notes

1. Wendy Schuman, "The Violent American Way of Life," *Parents*, September, 1980, p. 69. Used by permission.
2. Ibid., p. 68.
3. Madlyn Resener, "Burnout: The New Stress Disease," *Harper's Bazaar*, August, 1979, p. 36.
4. Schuman, p. 70.
5. Ibid., p. 69.
6. Ibid., p. 70.
7. J.L. Barkas, *The Help Book* (New York: Charles Scribner's Sons, 1976), pp. 65–67.

8

Just to Get Away

"There's just no use. Things will never change. I will be a prisoner to this job until the day I die," said Sally Weese, a forty-year-old nurse.

She had grown to despise her job at the University Hospital. It wasn't because of the money that she hated her job. The hospital paid well. In fact, that was the reason she had chosen nursing as a career. She hated her job because the pressure and anxiety were more than she could stand. When Sally came home from work, she could not turn off the headaches, tension, and bitterness which developed at work. Her husband John and her two children saw her growing more distant each day. John thought Sally was having an affair with another man. He could not explain her coldness and lack of communication toward him any other way. He had no idea that she was burning out because of stress.

Sally began asking herself some questions which she could not answer. As she drove to work every day she asked, "Sally, who are you? What are you? Where are you going?" Sally's inner self could never answer those questions. Those three questions seemed always to surface in her mind whenever she was alone.

One day while driving home on the freeway, Sally had the urge to take an off ramp to another interstate. *Chicago, this exit,* the sign read. For some reason she believed that the answer to those questions was somewhere in that direction and not at home. Sally took the exit and headed toward Chicago. *This is ridiculous,* she thought. *I'm in my nurse's uniform and only have fifty dollars in my purse.* Sally continued driving in spite of her own reasoning. The farther she went from that hospital and her home, the more free she felt. The feelings she was experiencing were comparable to the time when she was ten years old and rode her bike across the street determined "off limits" by her parents. She sensed all sorts of emotions which seemed to have been asleep for years. She felt a rush of excitement and even felt mischievous as she drove further and further away from the people and places she felt were binding her life.

After two stops for gasoline and one for food, Sally arrived in Chicago. But her excitement soon turned to fear as she saw the vastness of the city at night and the emptiness of her gas tank and billfold. Then she came to her senses and thought, *What am I doing to my family? They must be worried sick about me!* Sally pulled her car off the interstate at the next exit and nervously looked for a telephone so she could call John. *This area doesn't look very safe,* she thought. Finally she spotted a telephone booth. She dialed the operator and placed a collect call to her home. When John heard the request from the operator, he almost refused the call until he heard Sally yelling in the background.

"Sally, where are you? I was about to call the police!"

"John, I . . . don't know what is wrong with me. I just didn't want to come home or go back to that hospital. I'm in . . . Chicago."

"You're where?"

"In . . . Chicago."

"You mean that you just drove there! You weren't kidnapped or anything like that?"

"No, I just thought I could find some answers by coming here."

"Well, I've got an answer to a question. Is Sally nuts? Yes, indeed! Where are you in Chicago?"

"I really don't know. Wait a minute! I see a sign down the street. It says *Calvary Rescue Mission*. It's right off the Calumet Expressway at the Lincoln Highway exit. You can see the sign from the highway. I'll be there. Please come and get me, John."

"I'll be there and don't you leave that place."

Sally drove her car down to the building with the large red sign. Under the words *Calvary Rescue Mission* were the words *Jesus Saves*. She didn't quite understand what *Jesus Saves* meant, but she knew she was a good candidate for a rescue.

As she opened the door she noticed that something like a church service was in progress. She quietly entered and sat down in the last row of chairs in the back. Sally had gone to church some during her youth, but she had no time for it after she married John. Raising a family and working full time at the hospital was too much. She did not want any more demands. Sally thought, *I'll just wait here until John comes to get me. I guess I can tolerate what they want me to hear.*

There were only about twenty people in a room which seated fifty or more. Most of the people there were derelicts. As Sally looked at a woman in front of her she noticed that she wore a tattered dress and black tennis shoes. Beside her was a shopping bag which probably contained all her earthly goods.

When the singing stopped and the preacher stepped to the pulpit, Sally thought, *Well, here comes a sermon on drinking and laziness.* But Sally was surprised as the preacher, who must have been at least sixty, began to speak softly to everybody in that room. He started his message by explaining that sin is the reason why people have problems. He began at the beginning with Adam and Eve. He explained why and how their sin caused every human to inherit a sinful nature. He spoke about sin being rebellion against God's will and standards. He stressed the fact that no one can please God without acceptance of Jesus Christ as personal Savior. He explained how Jesus died on the cross to take the sinner's place. He promised that if any person in that room would turn from his or her sins, acknowledge God's grace, and ask Christ to be the Lord of his or her life, things would be different. He said, "Things will be different at home, at work, and especially in here," as he pointed to his heart. "Are you ready? Do you want a new life? Then please come down here now. I will pray with you as you ask Christ to be your Savior," said the preacher.

Sally thought, *He has given me the answers to those questions which have been bothering me for so long.* She had never considered herself a sinner bound for an eternity in hell. She had not even slightly connected her work and home problems with sin in her life. But now it was clear. God was speaking to her through this preacher, and she had to respond. Something had to change in her life, and now she knew what. Sally needed someone to give her freedom from guilt, forgiveness for her sins, and guidance through life. She believed that Jesus could do that.

Sally walked to the front and said to the preacher, "Read that verse again about things changing." The preacher turned in his Bible to Second Corinthians 5:17 and read, "Therefore if any man be in Christ, he is a new creature: old things are passed away; behold, all things are become new."

Sally asked, "Is that verse for women too?"

"Yes, it is!"

"Then that is what I want. If I don't have a change in my life, then I'm not sure if I even want to live anymore."

The preacher and Sally prayed right there in the front of the room, before the other people. Their presence did not seem to matter to her. The preacher helped her as she asked for God's forgiveness and prayed that Christ might come into her life and make that much-needed change. Sally experienced a peace within herself that things were now right between herself and God, and that things were going to become right at home and work.

A few hours later, John arrived with a friend. The friend drove Sally's car back while John and Sally went home in his car. Sally shared with John all the feelings that had caused her to do what she did. She also told him about the wonderful thing which had happened to her at the rescue mission. John dismissed her experience as another of her off-balance antics.

Sally became active in a strong Bible-believing church in her community. Through its minister and lay people, she was able to find much needed counsel. Sally's life was really different now. John noticed that there was a sense of joy, warmness, and peace about her that he had never seen before. This change in Sally's life and the warm outreach of her church was so impressive to her family that her children received Jesus Christ as personal Savior.

Life did not become problem-free for Sally and her family. John was still skeptical of her newfound faith. But things were different. Always before, Sally would worry and argue when problems arose. She learned to seek God's guidance and depend upon His strength in her job and in her marriage. God had promised Sally a change, and He certainly kept His Word. Sally's stress-related behavior had been transformed by the power of God.

Getting at the Root Level

It has been pointed out in Chapter 6 that most people who burn out are of a Type A behavior pattern. In studying that pattern an obvious element is an attitude of self-sufficiency. Most people—even Christians—who burn out believe that they can solve their own problems, give self-direction, and meet all their own needs. This self-sufficiency temperament springs forth from our fallen nature.

Every human being has a disposition to do what self wants rather than what God desires. The seeds of sin—pride, selfishness, self-pity—are planted in the fertile soil of our fallen nature. Those attitudes grow into actions of rebellion against God. The fallen nature leads people to seek careers for worldly gain or for personal pride. It is never satisfied. It demands so much but only gives temporal pleasures. One easily becomes enslaved to the demands of the fallen nature. It is like an extortionist whose greed is never satisfied with the blackmail money and who gives little in return.

Because of Sally's estrangement from God, daily demands were making her life miserable wherever she was. She had no joy in life at work or at home. It is not uncommon for people to one day try to escape from sin-related problems as Sally did. But running away will not help. You cannot run away from your fallen nature any more than you can run away from your shadow.

God has provided the only way to take care of the fallen nature and its ungodly behavior. A new nature through Jesus Christ is the only way to turn the problem of burnout around.

Dr. Henry Brandt, one of the leading Christian psychologists in America, once stated to a group of ministers that if his patients would not accept Jesus Christ, he could not help them. He knew of no cure in the realm of psychology for all of man's behavior problems, but in Jesus Christ he had found the answer.[1]

Burnout is just another symptom of the deep-rooted problems caused by a rebellious, fallen nature. Take, for example, the burnout symptoms of anger and self-pity. Where do these emotions originate? In the fallen nature. The fallen nature will not surrender any material possessions or personal rights to God. So the root cause develops into problems such as greed for money and power. The root problem then surfaces as wrong priorities, bitterness, insensitivity, stealing, cheating, and self-pity. Burnout cannot be treated on the surface; it must be treated at the root level. This is where God will work, if He is asked to do so.

The fallen nature is beyond repair. Nothing can be done to patch it up. Like Humpty Dumpty, it cannot be put back together again. When our parents Adam and Eve chose to disobey God, their nature fell from a state of obedience to disobedience (see Gen. 3). God, being holy, could no longer maintain a relationship with them because of their fallen nature. They were cast from the Garden of Eden to suffer the consequence of sin, which is spiritual and physical death. But God had a plan by which to bridge the gap created by Adam and Eve.

The second person of the Godhead came to earth and took upon Himself our humanity. God became man in Christ Jesus. This union of God and man means Jesus Christ assumed everything we are, save

126

for sin. He gathered together a small nucleus of followers and instructed them in the way in which this damage of the human race can be repaired. He then gave His life as payment for the sins of humanity, was buried, and on the third day rose victoriously over death. He then ascended to heaven and is now seated at the right hand of the Father.

The third person of the Godhead, the Holy Spirit, has been sent to the earth to expand the ministry of Christ all over the world. The Holy Spirit, among His many ministries, brings within the repentant sinner a new nature. This new nature is our personal union with Jesus Christ: God living in the heart of the Christian.

What about the old nature? Does it die or is something done with it? When the repentant sinner turns to God and receives Jesus into his or her life through the person of the Holy Spirit, the old, fallen nature is crucified (see Rom. 6:6). This crucifying of the old, fallen nature is a passive act on our part. It has been done for the Christian.

Some Christians who burn out wonder why it happened to them, since they have Christ in their lives. The answer is we are not perfect yet, though Christ has saved us. We still struggle with sin. The Bible says, "Likewise reckon ye also yourselves to be dead indeed unto sin, but alive unto God through Jesus Christ our Lord. Let not sin therefore reign in your mortal body, that ye should obey it in the lusts thereof" (Rom. 6:11,12).

The more sin is allowed to reign as king of the Christian's life, the more the problems characterized by that old nature will continue. Reckoning oneself dead to sin involves continual submission to God in all things. The unrepentant heart wants only to seek its own way, which is the way of trouble. The new nature desires only to seek God's perfect will, which is the way of peace. Allowing a fluctuating rule by first sin and rebellion, then by Christ, and then back again will produce instability in all aspects of life. Such fluctuation can cause a Christian to have joy one day and depression the next. This rollercoaster-type Christianity is not what God wants for His children.

God wants His children to be completely controlled by the Holy Spirit. He calls this act of complete control, the filling of the Holy Spirit. The indwelling of the Holy Spirit in the believer and His filling will produce amazing changes in the Christian.

> Being "born again" is a supernatural experience and as such should have a supernatural effect upon an individual. The degree of modification in a person's temperament will be in direct proportion to the filling of his life with the Holy Spirit. The Holy Spirit will automatically introduce new traits and characteristics into an individual's nature.[2]

God has set forth the plan for repairing the damage that we have brought into our own life. God has bridged the great gulf between Himself and us by the atonement for sin made by Jesus Christ. He has also provided a teacher and guide, the Holy Spirit, to live within every Christian. God wants humankind to enjoy life and work. But that enjoyment will never happen in your life unless you have entered into God's marvelous plan of salvation.

Trying to solve burnout on your own, without God, is like trying to get rid of weeds with a lawnmower. The yard looks great for a day or two, then the weeds are back. The weeds must be dealt with at the root level. God will deal with your burnout problems at the root level. Then He will enable you to repair the damage you have done to your family, friends, and job.

God wants every born-again believer to seek His power to change problem-causing temperaments.

> . . . so many people who pray "Lord, help me" never receive the help they expect. They want the Lord to take their fleshly (that is, carnal) abilities and add to them His power, making them strong enough to cope with the difficulties of life. But our selfish motivation is so abhorrent to God that He will not do that. He is not in the business of helping the humanly strong become stronger; rather He takes the weak and makes them strong *in Himself.*
>
> This is why failure can be a stepping stone if we respond to it in the right way. Anything that helps us see ourselves as the rebellious sinners which we really are is a help. When the mask of self-righteousness has been torn from us and we stand stripped of all of our accustomed defenses, we are candidates for God's generous grace.[3]

This truth became precious to me during my burnout. I came to look upon my failure not as a millstone hanging about my neck, but as a stepping stone under my feet. Did I develop this optimistic outlook overnight? Absolutely not! I had a difficult struggle to recover zeal for my work again.

Building Blocks

Here are four building blocks I discovered were helpful in restoring zeal for my ministry. They are basic principles of the Christian life, but they are easy to forget in times of stress. They will give meaning to your life and job no matter what type of work you do.

1. *Be filled with the Holy Spirit.* Ephesians 5:18 says, "And be not drunk with wine, wherein is excess; but be filled with the Spirit." We are not commanded to be "indwelt" with the Holy Spirit because He already has done that with every true believer (see Rom. 8:9). But every Christian is commanded to be filled (or controlled) by the Holy Spirit. Just as a person who is filled with wine is controlled by it, so the Christian who is filled with the Holy Spirit will be controlled by the Holy Spirit. God wants *complete* control!

Examine your heart daily to see in what private areas you do not want God's control. Your old nature works through these private areas to bring about discouragement, self-pity, and a critical spirit. Let Christ be the Lord of all your life. Let Him direct your thoughts, feelings, and actions (see 2 Cor. 10:5).

I believe one reason Christians burn out is because, like Peter walking on the water, we take our eyes and faith off Christ and focus them on the stressful circumstances about us. Let God's Spirit have His way with you.

2. *Forgive and forget.* I made an interesting discovery while interviewing victims of burnout. All of them had been hurt by remarks and deeds perpetrated by their employers. But the ones who had

forgiven and forgotten had a peaceful, loving attitude and a hopeful outlook on life. The others were just the opposite. Their unwillingness to forgive those who had hurt them caused their own lives to be bitter and cynical.

One burned out pastor who is now in another profession told me, "I could write a book about all the hurt I received. I'd rather not talk about it." That man will never recover from his burnout until he stops hating those people who injured him.

Colossians 3:13 says, ". . . if any man have a quarrel against any: even as Christ forgave you, so also do ye." Does God still remember your sin? Absolutely not! It is gone as far as the east is from the west (see Ps. 103:12). God holds no grudges, so why should we? Turn that hatred into a desire to see others blessed. Pray not for vengeance, but pray for your enemies so they might be blessed by God as you have been.

3. *Grow in the grace and knowledge of Jesus Christ.* Burnout caused me to have some mixed emotions. Since people were a major factor in my burnout, I wanted to be alone. Yet when I was alone, I sensed a strong need for friendship.

Thank God for the dear saints of His church. How thankful I am for fellow Christians who saw my need, even when I was silent. The wisdom, counsel, and ministering spirit of the church was crucial to my recovery from burnout. There I found strength from the support of fellow believers. I also realized that the body of believers is gifted to minister *with* and *to* the pastor. This was my greatest discovery! I was not alone in my struggle to overcome burnout—and I am not called to work alone in the ministry.

I also found strength from the study of God's Word. One day I was reading that familiar verse, Romans 8:28, "And we know that all things work together for good to them that love God, to them who are the called according to his purpose." I had quoted those words to myself many times during my burnout, but they never gave me the assurance that I needed.

Then I noticed verse 29: "For whom he did foreknow, he also did predestinate to be conformed to the image of his Son, that he might be the first-born among many brethren." Suddenly, I saw the reason I had to undergo the trauma of burnout. God was "conforming" me to the image of Jesus Christ. I had to experience the pressure of the Master Potter's hand upon me. Some faulty foundations first had to be removed. I had to be remolded into what He wanted me to be.

If I had chosen to avoid the family of God and neglect God's Word, I am certain I would not have recovered from burnout with the peace and positive attitude I have today.

4. *Exercise the trinity of graces.* The trinity of graces is faith, hope, and love (see 1 Cor. 13:13). Burnout damaged my attitude toward these three graces. My faith was not growing, my hope was but a glimmer, and my love was not Christ-like. I only loved those who loved me. I tried to forget those people who did not care for me. To me, the world was divided in two camps: those for me and those against me.

But after I allowed God's Spirit to have full control of my life again, after I forgave and asked forgiveness, and after I began to grow again in the grace and knowledge of Jesus Christ, these three graces took on new meaning in my life.

Faith

Before I burned out, my faith for salvation was in Christ, but my faith for my ministry was mostly in myself. I believed that those who were well educated, had attended the latest seminar programs, and had trained a competent staff could not fail—myself included.

God had to teach me that His ways are higher than my ways. His results may be different from the goals I plan. I had to learn that *He* is the Motivator; He is the Designer; I am only called to obey.

My faith in Christ is stronger now. My family and I have taken steps of faith that would have overwhelmed us years ago. Now we know that God will provide and care for us. We know that His eternal purpose is coming to pass through our lives.

Hope

My hope was also dimmed by burnout. My hope for the second coming of Christ and His eternal kingdom was not harmed the slightest. I used to hope it would happen soon and release me from the anguish of burnout!

But my hope for great things to happen in my life was all but gone. The zeal, enthusiasm, great plans, and excitement of the pastoral ministry dwindled away. Each hurt, each problem, and each trial whittled away my dreams a chip at a time.

It took the tender loving counsel of the people in my church to reestablish my hope. I learned that God did not lead me into the ministry to build mammoth cathedrals with standing room only! My hopes were in those realms early in my ministry. My hopes are now set on being faithful to God, using the opportunities He gives me, and being a *part*—not the determining factor—in adding new members to the family of God. If God decides to bless my ministry greatly, then all the glory will go to Him. But if I'm to be like 90–95 percent of my fellow pastors—average—then fine. My hope is in Christ who strengthens me.

Love

Burnout caused me to fully examine the meaning of love. According to First Corinthians 13:13, love is the greatest of these graces. Love is the greatest because it is the way in which we demonstrate what we believe. Love is a sacrificial, nonreciprocal way of saying, "I care about you." God demonstrated His love for us when He allowed His only begotten Son to die for our sins.

When I developed some enemies in the ministry, I was devastated. I thought, *This is not the way it is supposed to be. I am a nice guy and true to God's Word. What is there about me to dislike?* I began to dislike those people who disliked me! This unscriptural attitude fueled my burnout. I soon discovered that I was catering to those people who did not resist my programs and avoiding those who did. I surrounded myself with people who cared for me and isolated myself from the people who did not. I knew that this attitude was wrong, but I reasoned it was my only way of survival.

Then God convicted me of the sin of respect of persons. I was not allowing God to use me completely as an instrument of His love. God reminded me of this one day as I was standing in the check-out line of a discount department store. The female floor manager was giving the female cashier a tongue-lashing for not doing something right. It was the cashier's first day on the job. As the floor manager walked away still cursing, the cashier said, "I love you." I found out that this Christian clerk really meant what she said. She loved her oppressive floor manager! She was being used as an instrument of God's love.

My prayer has been, "Lord, love through me the unlovely as well as the lovely, the poor as well as the rich, and the sour as well as the sweet."

These are the building blocks for restoration from burnout. I found them to be true and practical, and God makes them available to all who will use them.

Notes

1. Tim LaHaye, *Spirit-Controlled Temperament* (Wheaton, Ill.: Tyndale House, 1975), p. 8.
2. Ibid., p. 126.
3. Erwin W. Lutzer, *Failure: The Back Door To Success* (Chicago: Moody Press, 1976), pp. 94,95.

9

An Honest Perspective

The phrase "You can't see the forest for the trees" is certainly applicable to the burned out worker. His problems seem so great and so numerous that he has no idea where to start repairing the damage done. How does a burned out worker get an honest perspective of his problems? After all, the continual stress will only dim his perspective! What is the answer?

Step out of the stress press and see where, with God's help, you can break it. This is not easy. But the victim of burnout *must* arrange to take some time off from his job (that is, if he still has a job!). This retreat has a dual purpose: first, to escape the destruction of stress, and second, to gain an honest perspective of one's job and its problems. This retreat can be made possible by utilizing your next vacation or, if possible, requesting a leave of absence. (Some people even work at a low-stress job during the leave of absence. This arrangement may not be allowed by some employers.)

A quick word of advice, however: *Don't quit your job*

in order to step out of the stress cycle. Unemployment causes greater stress! That additional pressure and uncertainty will prevent you from gaining an honest perspective of whatever caused your burnout in the first place.

The important thing is to get alone with God for this time of self-examination. This should be done in a place where you can spend a day or even several days in prayer and Bible study. You may elect to go alone, or bring your spouse along. This should be a time of identifying problems and waiting upon God for the answers.

The Bible encourages us to "Wait on the LORD: be of good courage, and he shall strengthen thine heart: wait, I say, on the LORD" (Ps. 27:14) and God "will instruct thee and teach thee in the way which thou shalt go: I will guide thee with mine eye" (Ps. 32:8). Ask God, through the Holy Spirit, to help you identify the problems with yourself and at work which have led to your burnout. God has promised to guide you. He will never go back on His Word.

Looking Inward

Here are some basic questions of self-examination which should be answered before going back to work.

1. *Do I expect more from my job than it can deliver?* As was said earlier, unrealistic expectations are a leading cause of burnout. What did you think your job would bring to your life? Good pay, security, happiness, success, and a sense of achievement? Did your em-

ployer promise you all those things, or did you change your dreams into promises?

Be realistic about benefits of the job. Don't look for a job to put into your life what only God can give. When you are doing God's perfect will at work, seeking His ways and obeying His commands, you are doing your best. This knowledge brings peace and satisfaction with your work.

2. *Do I live just to work?* Work is an honorable thing. God has commanded that we work and not be slothful (see Prov. 14:23). Work is essential to the demonstration of faith in God: "But if any provide not for his own, and specially for those of his own house, he hath denied the faith, and is worse than an infidel" (1 Tim. 5:8). Work is an obligation that every Christian has to God. The pay generated from it is to be used to maintain God's work here on earth, provide for one's family, and help those in need. But work is an obligation, not an obsession.

People burn out because they become obsessed with their work. This is especially true in "full-time Christian work." Missionaries are so bound to certain goals that they become the master, not God. Some youth workers are involved sixteen hours per day and seven days a week. When they are home, the conversation with the family is usually ministry-related. The lives of many pastors and their family are so permeated with "the church" that there is no escaping it.

No matter what kind of work you are in, establish working hours as much as possible. *Make appointments* for yourself to relax with your family. Don't break those appointments except in an emergency. Make sure your home is a haven of rest. Leave the job at the place of work. Don't accept phone calls or wear your beeper during supper or family devotional times. Never develop the attitude that you are *indispensable* and the work *needs* you.

3. *Am I qualified and capable of doing the work expected of me?* Credentials do not mean competence. The college degree on the wall does not say that this person is *able*. That degree states that the person whose name is on this paper has received the information and skills which are necessary to perform a task. Ability is yet another question!

Many college graduates enter a job within the scope of their training with little ability to accomplish the assigned work. There is a fear on the part of the graduate that if he says he can't do the work, he will not get the job. This constant fear of being incapable of the work is enough stress to set off burnout.

Very few employers specify in writing what they expect of their employees. If you are working in an ambiguous job description, then approach your employer about it. Ask him or her to define your job description clearly and to set goals to be met, in writing. Then work out a realistic agreement. Very few churches or Christian organizations have a written list of job duties for their workers. Sometimes they only say, "As the Spirit leads. . . ." How can anyone measure achievement without a standard? Every job needs to be described in detail so that there are no misunderstandings.

4. *Does success from my previous job drive me to push*

for success in my present one? If so, you are measuring your achievements with an inaccurate standard. No two jobs are identical, not even if they are in the same company or department. The expectations of Job A might have been met easily. Success was not that difficult to achieve. But if the expectations of Job B are not defined but are different from Job A, then success in Job B will not be found. For example, success at Job A might have been demonstrated by monetary gain to the company. Success at Job B might be demonstrated by unity between management and labor. Those results are quite different.

The success syndrome is a particular bane to Christians. For example, Bob had a successful pastorate which was demonstrated numerically by a growth in attendance from eighty-five to two hundred fifty people over a five-year period. God later led Bob to another church, which only had one hundred and twenty-five people in attendance. After four years o' hard work applying the same principles as in the previous church, Bob resigned. He quit because he felt he had failed. After four years the attendance was still only one hundred and twenty-five. But what Bob failed to see was the unity, love, and spiritual maturity which his teaching had brought to that church. Bob used a faulty standard for success and deemed himself a failure.

5. *What do I think of myself?* Every person has a mental picture of oneself. That picture is either good, mediocre, or bad. This mental picture affects behavior, attitudes, productivity at work, and success in life. Tim LaHaye, a noted counselor and speaker,

comments about self-image in his book, *How To Win Over Depression:*

> Thoughts produce feelings and feelings produce actions; consequently your self-image thoughts definitely affect your actions, negatively or positively.
>
> One who maintains a self-confident image of himself will perform to his maximum ability, but the insecure person who lacks self-confidence will not.
>
> Most people make a singular mistake regarding self-image: they allow other people's opinions to influence their view of themselves. Quite to the contrary, what a person thinks of himself will affect what other people think of him.[1]

When you realize that your self-image is directly related to how others treat you at work, you will make sure that it is positive. Keep in mind, however, that a positive self-image does not mean pride or superiority.

Shaping Your Self-Image

LaHaye gives three good reasons why you should not let your fellow workers shape your self-image:

1) You should accept yourself as God values you, not as other people do.
2) You cannot always judge what people think about you by their appearance or actions, for they may be concentrating on something else entirely.
3) What other people think of you is usually a reflection of your own self-image. If you feel inferior, you emit the feeling of inferiority, and consequently others will look upon you as inferior.[2]

Determine the area in your life where you lack self-confidence. Self-image problems are usually found in these four areas: first, in one's own appearance; second, in one's own abilities; third, in one's own family; and fourth, in one's own environment.[3] If you lack self-confidence because of your appearance, your abilities, your family's reputation, or your economic status, change these things! If that is beyond your power, then ask for God's grace to accept these things as His will.

Some commentators believe that the apostle Paul suffered from poor eyesight. This affliction undoubtedly gave Paul a self-image problem. He prayed to God three times for Him to remove this problem from his life (see 2 Cor. 12:8). God's answer was not what Paul wanted to hear, but he knew it was the right answer. God said, ". . . My grace is sufficient for thee: for my strength is made perfect in weakness . . ." (2 Cor. 12:9). Paul then answered God with these words, ". . . Most gladly therefore will I rather glory in my infirmities, that the power of Christ may rest upon me" (2 Cor. 12:9).

Above all, change your attitude in these four areas. The change will help your self-image and self-confidence. This positive image in turn will affect the way your fellow workers and clients treat you. A strong self-image elicits respect from others. What you can't change, turn over to God. He knows our needs and has promised to supply all of them (see Phil. 4:19).

6. *How do I feel toward those people at work who have been abusive and hateful toward me?* People who burn out usually become bitter toward fellow workers and

clients. Bitterness produces hurt in them; which in turn causes them to reciprocate with more bitterness. The cycle can be vicious. What should be your response as a Christian when abused? Jesus said, ". . . Love your enemies, bless them that curse you, do good to them that hate you, and pray for them which despitefully use you, and persecute you" (Matt. 5:44).

You might think, *That is impossible, I can't love those people who have hurt me so much!* You are right! *You* cannot love them of yourself, but Christ will empower you to love them. Love is a fruit of the Holy Spirit (see Gal. 5:22). When you allow the Spirit to have full control of your life, you can love and forgive people who have mistreated you. ". . . The love of God is shed abroad in our hearts by the Holy Ghost which is given unto us" (Rom. 5:5).

This question must be answered and resolved before you go back to work. Make special arrangements to meet those who have hurt you. Explain to them what has happened in your life spiritually. Ask for their forgiveness, forgive them, and forget that the difficulty ever happened.

If you put off dealing with bitterness and hatred, the burnout stress will begin again as soon as you start back to work. Don't put this action off until a more convenient day. "Satan cares not how spiritual your intentions, or how holy your resolutions, if only they are fixed for tomorrow!"[4]

7. *Am I working where God wants me?* This question, of course, is filled with many other questions. After a person accepts Jesus Christ as Savior and Lord, life

itself takes on a different perspective. Paul spoke of this different perspective when he said, "For to me to live is Christ . . ." (Phil. 1:21). Christ is the center of the Christian's life. Everything revolves around and is fixed to Him.

If you chose your career and place of employment before you became a Christian, you must again seek God's guidance concerning your work. I remember clearly the fellow seminarians who were former attorneys, accountants, and school teachers. These men, after their conversion, asked God for guidance concerning their careers and place of employment. God did not give them inner peace about their present careers. He led them into the ministry. This is certainly not to say every Christian will be led into a pastorate. God has directed Christian people into ministries of medicine, nursing, teaching, sales work, and journalism. These jobs are not God's *second best* for His children. God leads Christians to His very best for each one. *Being where God wants you* is His very best for your life.

This question was put last in the seven, because some Christians are quick to say, "God wants me to change jobs," rather than facing up to and dealing with problems.

Think about how Paul admonished the Corinthians:

> Every one should remain in the state in which he was called. Were you a slave when called? Never mind. But if you can gain your freedom, avail yourself of the opportunity. For he who was called in the Lord as a

slave is a freedman of the Lord. Likewise he who was free when called is a slave of Christ. You were bought with a price; do not become slaves of men (1 Cor. 7:20–23 RSV).

Paul desired for the Corinthians to consider their occupations—even slavery—prayerfully, seeking God's will slowly, earnestly, and thoroughly. Never give the credit to God for leading you in that which is nothing more than a cowardly action. You will do more harm than good.

If you have answered these questions in a positive way and resolved the problems, then work with this seventh question. Ask God for His wisdom. Seek the counsel of your pastor and other mature Christians. Move ahead slowly but obediently. You will not find a true sense of peace with yourself unless you are working where God wants you.

Notes

1. Tim LaHaye, *How To Win Over Depression* (Grand Rapids, Mich.: Zondervan, 1976), pp. 138–140.
2. Ibid., p. 140.
3. Bill Gothard, *Institute In Basic Youth Conflicts*, 1975, p. 1.
4. Eleanor Doan, *Sourcebook for Speakers* (Grand Rapids, Mich.: Zondervan, 1968), p. 300.

10

Decisions, Decisions!

What shall I do now? This was one of several questions I asked myself after recovering from burnout. Shall I remain where I am and continue in the work that burned me out? Shall I go elsewhere and seek a new pastorate? Shall I seek a new ministry in a different area of service? My mind was filled with questions but no answers.

Life is filled with questions which have to be answered. Some of these are simple enough: What time shall I get up in the morning? What shall I wear? Shall I take my lunch or buy it at work?

Life would be pleasant indeed if these simple decisions were the only ones we had to make. But more than a few decisions result in long-term consequences. Whom will I marry? What type of work will I do? Shall I buy or rent a home? Shall I buy a new or used car? Shall I join the church I attend?

Nearly everybody is looking for some sort of direction in decision making. Some people seek help from horoscopes, fortune-tellers, palm readers, and spiritist mediums—all of which are condemned by the

Bible as not being pleasing to God (see Deut. 18:10–12). Other people seek guidance from professional counselors and guidance clinics. Dr. Eric H. Marcus, a Los Angeles physician, made this interesting comment about decision making:

> As a therapist, whenever I work with someone who has come for help in making a decision, I focus first on the advantages of what she is doing rather than on what she wants to do. I ask her to consider, in detail, the advantages of not deciding. The primary payoff of this approach is to postpone the responsibility for the decision. If you postpone a decision, you can avoid taking a risk and facing the potential consequences. You cannot be responsible for an error in choosing the wrong path if you don't choose any path! Most of us would like to have some sort of guarantee that we will be choosing the "right" path and are unwilling to risk selecting the "wrong" one. The deeper issue is that there is no guarantee that any path is the "right" path.[1]

Is there no guarantee that there is a "right" path for every believer? Never! The Scriptures are permeated with divine directions concerning the right path for God's children. That path is known as God's will. The Bible commands that Christians develop an understanding of God's will: "See then that ye walk circumspectly, not as fools, but as wise, redeeming the time, because the days are evil. Wherefore be ye not unwise, but understanding what the will of the Lord is" (Eph. 5:15–17).

Decision making is an integral part of understanding what God's will is all about. The Christian's primary source of guidance is the One who knows tne future and has the ability to change it. Christians live in a world which He made, maintains, and moves to accomplish His ultimate purpose. He has a blueprint for every Christian: "For we are his workmanship, created in Christ Jesus unto good works, which God hath before ordained that we should walk in them" (Eph. 2:10). The "good works" mentioned in this verse are the results of God's working His will through us in every aspect of our lives.

This working of His will through the lives of believers is His blueprint. If you have ever tried to read a contractor's blueprints, you know that it takes some knowledge and training to read them correctly. The ame holds true in the reading of God's blueprint for our lives. His blueprint is not a mystical look into the tuture, but a solid peace about our lives today. The ability to determine that peace about God's blueprint takes knowledge and training.

Put Out the Fleece?

During the dispensation of the Mosaic Law, God chose to allow Israel to use physical objects, something like drawing straws, to determine His will. Some Christians choose this method of determining God's will because of the example set forth by Gideon.

Gideon was commissioned by God to smite the oppressive Midianites: "And the LORD looked upon him, and said, Go in this thy might, and thou shalt save Israel from the hand of the Midianites: have not I sent thee?" (Judg. 6:14). This command was God's will for Gideon. This was all Gideon should have needed. But because of his lack of faith, he wanted to see a physical sign of God's direction. So, he put a fleece on the ground and asked God to make it wet with dew and keep the ground dry, if this was His will. God did what Gideon asked. Gideon then asked for the reverse. He wanted a wet ground and a dry fleece! God accommodated Gideon's request again. Gideon received the sign that he wanted.

Is this a scriptural example to follow? No! God did not command Gideon to look for a sign. Are we ever commanded to seek after phenomenal and super-natural signs? Not in all the Scriptures are we commanded to seek God's will in this manner. But Jesus did have something to say about people who seek for signs: "A wicked and adulterous generation seeketh after a sign . . ." (Matt. 16:4). Christians who seek after signs for determining God's will are really acting like unbelievers who have no faith in God.

Since seeking after a sign is not the right way, what is the correct way to make a decision in agreement with God's blueprint? Reading God's blueprint correctly involves *knowledge* about the Holy Spirit and *training* as to how to apply what has been learned. How much knowledge does the average Christian have of the Holy Spirit? Not much. Some Christians even avoid the words *Holy Spirit* for fear of being branded an "extremist."

The Holy Spirit is the third Person of the Godhead, who personally indwells all believers (see Rom. 8:9). He is also the only teacher who knows the blueprint and how to read it (see 1 Cor. 2:10,11)! If you fail to recognize this valuable Teacher, then your decisions will be nothing more than shots in the dark.

Yielding to the Holy Spirit is a vital part of this knowledge. We are commanded: ". . . Present your bodies a living sacrifice, holy, acceptable unto God, which is your reasonable service. And be not conformed to this world: but be ye transformed by the renewing of your mind, that ye may prove what is that good, and acceptable, and perfect, will of God" (Rom. 12:1,2).

Pressure to Disobey

Glenn was a twenty-five-year-old seminary student with a wife and two small children. When he had sensed a strong leading from God to enter the ministry and attend seminary, he and his wife had prayed together, and she had been supportive of his decisions in the beginning of the venture.

But her faith began to falter when financial stresses became too much for her. In order to meet his tuition and household expenses, Glenn had to work at a job full time at night and then attend school during the day. His continual absence from home caused marital problems. Things continued to get worse. Then one day Glenn's wife gave him an ultimatum: "Quit school or I will divorce you!"

Glenn, being concerned for his marriage and family, left seminary and returned to his hometown to look for work. His spiritual life soon began to suffer. He became a pew-warmer. He became slack in his

Bible study and prayer. He gave God one hour per week of his time! Glenn remained unemployed for over a year. He prayed every day that God might reveal His will to him.

Where did Glenn go wrong? How might he have handled the situation differently? Could he pray to God for a "sign" after he dropped back to a mere pew-warmer? I would say not! God doesn't lay out such a blueprint as Glenn was living! God's plan is perfect; He is never the author of confusion. His plan is designed for our eternal good and for His glory.

An unyielding Christian is much like a rebellious student. The rebellious student believes that he can always choose the best way, always find the right path, and always do the right things without anyone's help. God's Word says, "O LORD, I know that the way of man is not in himself: it is not in man that walketh to direct his steps" (Jer. 10:23). The Holy Spirit—not us—knows the blueprint! Only when we recognize that He knows it and are willing to allow Him to instruct us in it, can our eyes be opened to know God's will.

Lewis Sperry Chafer, the former president and professor of theology at Dallas Theological Seminary, once said:

> One who is yielded to God must account himself in the will of God when he is unreservedly willing to do God's will. If the position one occupies in life or service is not what God desires, surely He can, providing that one is yielded, move him out into the place which He does choose. The will of God indeed

is not primarily a matter of a Christian's being in one place or another; it is rather of his being willing to do God's will. All else is then easily adjusted.[2]

Glenn was unwilling to yield to the Holy Spirit for fear that God was not able to keep his marriage and family together. Instead of making sure he and his wife were of one mind and praying earnestly, Glenn plunged on determinedly in his own strength. Finally, he allowed the difficult circumstances and the ultimatum from his wife to make the decision for him.

Every Christian must be willing to *let go and let God* do as He desires. This is the key to the knowledge of the Holy Spirit's work in decisions.

Four Practical Steps

Now comes the practical aspect, the training of the Christian to sense the Holy Spirit's leading. This training involves taking certain thoughtful steps, constantly seeking the Lord in prayer and His Word and being excruciatingly honest with yourself. These four steps, *interest, inquiry, inner peace,* and *instrumentation,* have proved to be most helpful to me and to those who have sought my counsel in this matter.

1. *Be aware of what you find interesting.* This is the way God directs! He puts within you an *interest* for a certain work that no other occupation will satisfy. The Bible says, ". . . If a man desire the office of a bishop, he desireth a good work" (1 Tim. 3:1). Notice the emphasis God puts on *desire* or *interest* in the

work. God can put the desire in a Christian's heart for any kind of work, as long as it glorifies Him and is within His blueprint. God would not put within you a desire to be a prostitute or a bank robber. Those occupations certainly do not glorify God, nor would they be within His purpose for eternal good.

How does God give us this desire? His Word says, "Delight thyself also in the LORD; and he shall give thee the desires of thine heart" (Ps. 37:4). He gives it when we seek Him. One outgrowth of that is becoming involved with God's people. A young Christian man who loved music and electronics could not sense where God wanted him in a job until he became very active in his church. There he met a man who introduced him to the business of recording gospel music. He became interested to a degree that he knew that this was God's leading. He entered that business, and God is blessing him greatly.

But how did this young man know that *God* was leading? That is where the next step leads us.

2. *Be aware of the need for inquiry.* Ask God about your desires and your decisions, and ask Christians around you. God made us to be rational beings. We are made in the image of God with intellect, emotion, and will. The great theologian Augustus H. Strong once said, "Intellect is the soul knowing; sensibility is the soul feeling; will is the soul choosing. In every act of the soul, all the faculties act."[3]

The Holy Spirit can guide all your faculties to work together in decision making. He can give the necessary discernment in the gathering of information. He can control the emotions so as not to allow them to bring motivation from feelings instead of facts. He can give the ability to weigh out all the information, combine it with the interest, and come to a conclusion which is within God's blueprint.

The counsel of your pastor and lay church leaders is an important part of seeking God's will. I remember a Christian businessman in our church who came to me one day for counsel. He said, "Pastor Perry, I have been the manager at the plant for ten years. I want to start my own business. I have the money and the experience. All I need is the go ahead from God. How do I know whether He wants me to start my own business or not?"

I went through the four steps with him. We talked for about two hours concerning the matter. We prayed, and then he went home.

About a month later I asked him, "What did you decide?"

He said, "I decided to stay with the firm. I had no peace about it. Am I glad I listened to God! I found out yesterday that if I had invested my money in the venture I proposed, I would have lost it all!"

3. *Be aware that God gives inner peace about decisions.* Let us say, for example, that you have burned out of your job as a public high school teacher. You are walking in obedience to God's commands, you are yielded to Him—and you are interested in starting a home for runaway teenagers. You have gathered a mountain of information and have prayed about it for six months. Should you consider the home just a "hare-brained idea" and go back to teaching, or should you attempt to take on this venture?

"How can I know for sure?" is usually the question at this point.

The Bible has an answer! "Let the peace of God rule in your hearts, to the which also ye are called in one body; and be ye thankful" (Col. 3:15). The word *rule* in its original form meant "to umpire." When the umpire calls a play at a ball game, it does not matter how many jeers come from the crowd, or even how many bottles and cans are thrown at him. When he makes his decision, the matter is settled. When the Holy Spirit gives that perfect peace about the decision (in this case, the home for teenagers), then nothing should move you from it.

What is this perfect peace? It is an absence of uneasiness. It is a calm in the midst of a storm of difficulties. Paul had experienced this peace many times, and he exhorted the believers at Philippi to seek it also when he said, "And the peace of God, which passeth all understanding, shall keep your hearts and minds through Christ Jesus" (Phil. 4:7).

4. *Be aware of the importance of instrumentation.* Put to work what God has laid upon your heart. Larry has made the decision to work in a church-planting ministry in Central America. He has been through the *interest, inquiry,* and *inner peace,* but he cannot get to the *instrumentation.* He is always working on what he is going to do when he gets there. He has been doing that for five years. In the meantime he continues to work at odd jobs while trying to establish a perfect work plan. Unless Larry takes a step of faith, he will always be planning, not producing.

Instrumentation is faith in action. James said ". . . I

will show thee my faith by my works" (James 2:18). Stepping out in faith might mean a great deal of sacrifice of worldly possessions, power, and prestige. It could be that those things are a detriment to your life anyway. Look to this step as the opening of a door to new opportunities to serve God. Don't consider this action a leap in the dark. We are children of light, not darkness.

Will God's blessing be a confirmation that you have made the right decision? The confirmation by God comes back in the third step with *inner peace.* God may decide, in His infinite wisdom, not to show physical signs of blessing right away upon your endeavor. Stand firm in your step of faith, keep your heart open to the Holy Spirit, and don't allow doubts, fears, or criticism to persuade you to draw back from God's leading in your life.

These are four areas in which every believer must be trained in order to be led by the Holy Spirit. Is this system easier than the Old Testament system of lot-casting? No, it is not *easier.* But it is *better.* God has given you an active part in making decisions which will affect you for the rest of your life.

Decisions, decisions! Everybody must make them. But only the child of God has the opportunity to make them in the right way.

Notes

1. Eric H. Marcus, M.D., "Decision-Making Without Fear," *Vogue*, May, 1980, p. 156. Copyright © by The Condé Nast Publications, Inc. Used by permission.
2. Lewis Sperry Chafer, *Systematic Theology* (Dallas: Dallas Seminary Press, 1973), Vol. 6, p. 228.
3. Augustus H. Strong, *Systematic Theology* (Valley Forge, Penn.: Judson Press, 1969), p. 505.

11
Starting Over

Americans would rather switch than fight! That is, switch careers rather than fight the frustrations of working in boredom or in the state of burnout. How many Americans are switching careers? A survey by the U.S. Government reported that nearly a third of all Americans may change careers over a five-year period.[1]

What causes this transition among the workers of America? There are really two reasons:

> One involves economic forces which cause jobs to disappear. Teachers may decide their careers are in jeopardy because of a shrinking school age population.
>
> But the second reason is equally important; it centers on the change in social values we've been seeing in recent years. The individual looking for personal growth and development these days no longer is satisfied to stay in one job for years on end, no matter how large the paycheck or secure the situation.[2]

As said earlier, most career changes are caused by job boredom, frustration, loss of autonomy, or lack of advancement opportunities. All of these factors contribute to burnout, so most career changes should be understood as related to burnout. Most people simply change careers before burnout actually takes place.

Who are the people who believe that starting over is better than the spectre of living in the ashes? They are men and women about thirty-five years of age. But older workers are not exempted from switching careers. "Bernard Haldane Associates, pioneering professional career-management experts, estimates that in any one year, between 35,000 and 37,000 Americans over age 55 change careers."[3] What are their occupations? Workers with the most time and money invested in their careers switch less frequently. Fewer than 10 percent of lawyers, doctors, and pharmacists switch careers. But 58 percent of garage and gas station workers eventually change to another job. Forty percent of computer operators and 38 percent of broadcast announcers end up switching careers.[4]

In most instances, a career change is a choice. But in some cases, e.g. if a career disappears or if the burned out career is unsalvageable, then one must seek a new career. This chapter is designed for those people who have suffered burnout to the point their career is unsalvageable. Many recommendations will prove helpful to those who have the "itch to switch." However, a word of warning: *It is a fallacy to think that switching will make things better.* The grass is not always greener on the other side of the fence. You often end up simply exchanging one set of frustrations for another.

We should define "starting over" (a career change) as a switch to a completely new job having different tasks and requiring different skills. An example of starting over is the forty-three-year-old retail sales manager who was so frustrated with his seventeen years of hassles that he quit and became a maintenance man for a local hospital. Starting over is a complete turnabout from the previous career.

Answer These Questions First

Starting over is not an easy venture. The pressure of change and new demands is stressful, and can be harmful to mental, physical, and spiritual stamina. People involved in starting over need to follow some valuable principles. Let me offer a checklist of five questions.

1. *Have you counted the cost?* I'm speaking here not of the financial aspect, which will be mentioned in question three, but of the cost to you and your family's spiritual, mental, and physical health. Switching careers usually involves relocation. Moving results in all kinds of stress on the whole family. Friendships are uprooted, church ties must be reestablished, new schools must be endured—even grocery shopping will be trying for a time in unfamiliar surroundings.

Jesus spoke of counting the cost as being an action of common sense: "For which of you, intending to build a tower, sitteth not down first, and counteth the cost, whether he have sufficient to finish it. Lest haply, after he hath laid the foundation, and is not able to finish it, all that behold it begin to mock him, saying, This man began to build, and was not able to finish" (Luke 14:28–30).

There are many things which must be carefully considered while trying to count the cost. Does God want us there? (See chapter 10 for a review on decisions.) Will this change be harmful to my family? Will we like the new area? Will the children be able to adjust?

These are just a few of the many questions which need to be asked and answered. Sometimes the desire to escape is so great, the tendency is not to consider the rest of the family during a career change.

Count the cost! Maybe you can start over and still remain in your same geographic location. This solution is certainly less stressful. Are you willing to pay the high price of the spiritual, mental, and physical strain which switching careers requires?

2. *Do you know yourself?* This book has dealt extensively with this subject. What are your *real* motives for wanting a new career? Are you trying to escape the inevitable frustrations, pressures, or the boredom of a corporate job? Disappointments, struggles, occasional slumps come with the day-to-day living in any occupation, no matter how "right" it is for you. Once a man said to me, "I think I'll become a preacher. Why, you only work three hours a week giving those sermons." Ironically, the man made such a statement at a lengthy board meeting which was approaching the 11:00 P.M. hour. Envy is not limited to coveting your neighbor's new swimming pool. Many career changes stem from nothing more than coveting thy neighbor's career. Coveting is certainly a violation of God's commandments.

Make certain your motives are pure and directed by God. Don't try to fool others or yourself in pretending to want something just for the sake of escape. Many times God gets the credit for "leading" people away from careers that He formerly led them into taking. Strange indeed! Make certain that you are seeking God's will and not your own fleshly desires.

3. *Are you prepared to pay?* Career changes are costly. Most career consultants urge a financial reserve of at least one year's salary.[5] Does this advice contradict the promise of God found in Philippians 4:19? That promise reads "But my God shall supply all your need according to his riches in glory by Christ Jesus." This verse does not say *how* He will supply the needs but *by whom*. One year's salary in the bank should certainly be considered a provision from the Lord. This should be the Christian's attitude toward all temporal possessions.

The financial costs of career changes are astronomical. There are career consultant fees, educational instruction fees, moving expenses, possible period of unemployment, loss on selling the previous house, increased price on a new house, new tools or books needed, and many more. The change also might involve taking a drastic cut in salary because he or she is starting at the bottom again. The financial aspect of a career change quite often can cause a new career to go sour even before the first year honeymoon is over.

Are you willing to pay out a year's worth of income to start over? That money probably had some dreams behind it. Make certain that you have God's leading in money matters. Another vital requirement is that the whole family be in agreement with the way you are about to spend away their dreams.

My family was in total agreement concerning the decision to use our savings for a new start. My wife agreed to use the money which had been set aside to purchase a house some day. Our sixteen-year-old son Phillip had saved his money for six years to buy a car. He told us, "Dad and Mom, if we run out of money after we move, you can use my car money."

If there is no family unity in this matter, the consequences could turn up years later in the form of bitterness and resentment for spoiling somebody's dreams. Are you willing to pay the expensive price tag for a career change?

4. *What do you expect?* Do you expect your new career to be a land flowing with milk and honey? Do you expect to leave all those problems and frustrations behind with that despicable job? Remember, unrealistic expectations lead to burnout! On the other hand, don't be pessimistic and expect the worst. Be realistic about your work. Consider it as what it is supposed to be: your *livelihood*, not your *life*.

Don't expect to give your new work the same amount of energy you gave your first career twenty years ago. Be realistic about your age and your health. Don't expect more from yourself than you are mentally or physically able to give. Your ego may tell you to try to pace yourself with those "young whip per snappers," but your common sense should tell you differently.

Your job cannot give you happiness, peace, security, or any of the other attributes claimed by some employers. Your relationship with God will provide the happiness, peace, and security necessary for living an abundant life. Don't ever look to a job as a "deliverer." A job makes a poor master and a burned out worker makes even a poorer servant.

5. *How long is your patience?* The Bible says, ". . . tribulation worketh patience . . ." (Rom. 5:3). Tribulation means trouble. Patience is like a muscle—unless it is flexed it will atrophy. Tribulation builds patience.

It doesn't take long for the excitement of a career change to wear away. Then comes a time of letdown and disappointment. "Some who have gone through career changes report that they do not fully regain their confidence in themselves for a year or more."[6]

If you have been led by the Spirit to make a definite career change, then pray for God to lead you likewise in the exercising of patience. Patience is a fruit of the Spirit-filled life. God can produce patience within you to prevent frustration and to deal with problems at work.

We are told that God's children are "Strengthened with all might, according to his glorious power, unto all patience and long-suffering with joyfulness" (Col. 1:11). God will not bring any problem or tribulation upon you that is not for your good or His glory, and it will never be more than you can bear (see Rom. 8:28; 1 Cor. 10:13). "Let patience have her perfect work, that ye may be perfect and entire, wanting nothing" (James 1:4).

And as for Me . .

Starting over in a new ministry was a difficult decision for me and for all of us in the family. We counted the cost, examined our motives, prepared ourselves to sacrifice much financially, and set out for California. We had sensed God's leading about one specific location, and we had peace that it was his will.

We experienced four months of unemployment after we arrived. But God kept me busy with preaching opportunities practically every Sunday.

I enrolled in a computer programming school in order to develop a technical skill. (The job market was not interested in my theological education and skills.) And God later opened a position for me with a data processing consultant firm.

Then the pastor of the church we were members of passed away, and the board asked me to serve in that ministry. I am ministering there now.

God has been so good to us. Our unrealistic expectations are gone. We expect the trials and tribulations along with the blessings. We know that God will work through them to continue to conform us to the image of His dear Son.

And what about you? My hope is that my experience and observations will not be considered a formula for recovery from burnout, but instead will be recognized as a guide from one who has been through it and survived! If this book helps only one person to prevent or recover from burnout, I will consider my journey worth it all.

May the Lord bless you in your work.

Notes

1. Morton Yarmon, "7 Rules to Follow If You Change Your Job, *50 Plus,* August, 1979, p. 20.
2. "Switching Careers: How to Make It Work," *U.S. News and World Report,* March 10, 1980, p. 85.
3. Yarmon, p. 20.
4. Ibid.
5. Ibid., p. 21.
6. Ibid.